T0301231

SMARTER

SMARTER

10 lessons for a more productive and less-stressed life

E M AUSTEN

PIATKUS

PIATKUS

First published in Great Britain in 2024 by Piatkus

1 3 5 7 9 10 8 6 4 2

A CIP catalogue record for this book
is available from the British Library.

ISBN 978-0-34944-373-7

Printed and bound in Great Britain by
Clays Ltd, Elcograf S.p.A.

Papers used by Piatkus are from well-managed forests
and other responsible sources.

Piatkus
An imprint of
Little, Brown Book Group
Carmelite House
50 Victoria Embankment
London EC4Y 0DZ

An Hachette UK Company
www.hachette.co.uk

To my parents, for always reminding me that I could do anything.

To fourteen-year-old Emily. She endured.

To the girls and boys reading this: I hope you win the battles that you never tell anyone about.

CONTENTS

Introduction 1

1. Mornings 11
2. Message 55
3. Minutes 80
4. Mind(ful) 114
5. Manage 140
6. Modify 160
7. Marketing 172
8. Mastery 192
9. Move 208
10. Momentum 233

Conclusion 255

Acknowledgements 259

Notes 261

Index 265

INTRODUCTION

Welcome to the smarter you . . .

This is not for fans of bare-minimum Mondays or take-it-easy Tuesdays. It's for those who strive for success. For ambitious people wanting to do it all. Those who understand that you have to make a deposit to be able to make a withdrawal. For those who have skin in the game. For the overlooked. The under-appreciated. The full-timers and the 'not-quite-made-it-yet-ers'. The entrepreneurs. The enthusiasts. Those who are looking for a smarter way to do it.

As we begin, I'd like you to ask yourself three questions:

1. Why is it that your level of self-worth is tied to your level of productivity?
2. How often do you try to prove your value to others?
3. Why do you seek the approval and validation of others, and how much time do you spend doing it?

Smarter is here to tell you that ***you have more time than you think and you are much smarter than you realise.***

WHY THIS BOOK, WHY NOW, WHY ME?

Working hard is in my blood. I was raised to be competitive, to not take no for an answer and to understand the value of money. If I wanted cash to go to the sweet shop, I had to first clean the car. Dad and I picked samphire, and I sold it on the side of the road for £1 per bag during summer holidays in Norfolk. I babysat the children of my parents' friends when I was fourteen – sometimes earning £2 for a whole evening (those £2 coins were elite). I worked at our local tennis centre, restringing rackets and answering the phones when I was fifteen. I started a terrible blog at school and had a radio show at university, which turned into a podcast. I worked, unpaid, throughout my time at Manchester University, gaining experience in a number of different jobs. I started a company as an undergrad selling social media packages to local businesses to pay back my student loan. At twenty, I co-founded a talent management and PR agency, which I had intended to grow once I graduated. My business partner, however, drained our bank account and disappeared eight days after I was finally done with studying. Happy Graduation!

Despite the setback, my parents agreed that I had a good business plan and that I was young enough to start again. If I failed, I'd only be twenty-five, and I'd have enough experience under my belt to make me very employable. We sat around the kitchen table thinking of company names, wrote a mission statement, and the following day, I went to the high street bank to set up a business account. That business is now a multi-million-pound PR agency, working with brands including Red Bull, Abercrombie, Spanx, Huel, Grind and more.

While I was well versed in the importance of hard work, no one had ever explained to me the negative impact it could have on my life, if not managed well. The concept of smart working was not introduced to me in tandem with hard work. Rather, it has been something I have had to learn over my career.

I spent my university years miserable, anxious to find something I liked about myself, desperate to identify my passion, battling my weight and low self-esteem and feeling the need to succeed. I felt entirely untethered, with no idea where I was going to go, or what I was going to do. While I had a fire inside me, I had nowhere to direct it so it just burned me up. Everyone else seemed to be living their best life and on the surface it looked like I was living mine. I developed a talent for maintaining one public face and one private face. I had destructive patterns relating to food and sugar. I felt constantly jet-lagged. I assumed that the harder things were for me, the more successful I would be. Following an unsuccessful suicide attempt in my second year at university, I made a promise to myself that if I was going to live for another seventy years, it had to be different, or I just wouldn't survive.

I spent the next decade passionately committed to showing up for myself. To protect the fire I had lit, and to find a way for others to nurture their own embers. It hasn't been linear and it's certainly not been easy. But it was possible. The ups and downs of starting and scaling a multi-million-pound agency; navigating my way through a global pandemic; living with a formal diagnosis of PTSD, depression and OCD; healing after my mentor took his own life in my twenties; negotiating with bailiffs after my financial director at the time embezzled money from the company; losing 40 kilos after finally addressing my toxic relationship with food; recognising abusive relationships; living in the shadows; and rupturing a stomach ulcer – all of these things made my twenties a cocktail of confusing and personally challenging growth.

I've had the great privilege of working alongside some of the most successful people in the world, advising powerful and meaningful organisations, backing businesses and causes with people at the heart, and sharing my thoughts on how to find a smarter way through. I believe entirely that women in particular have had little choice but to subscribe to a narrative that puts them second. The pressures of having perfect families, being young forever, creating financial independence, managing male dominance, learning how to ask for more, excelling as mothers, CEOs, employees, friends, wives and caregivers, creates an exhausting expectation that asks – nay demands – us to give all that we have, all the time. As an ambitious and successful young woman, I reject entirely the idea that the way it has always been, is the way it needs to continue. From my experience I believe, with enormous passion, that we can have it all.

This book offers a carefully constructed ten-step programme to help avoid burnout and live life smarter, while still achieving your goals. It is not designed to replace the graft, the determination or the commitment, but to consider that success at all costs is not conducive to a happy life, and to challenge societal frameworks of success. Here are the key pillars of my Smarter Method:

- create your own definitions
- practise gratitude
- master the morning
- cultivate an abundant mindset
- identify and enforce healthy boundaries
- track energy not time
- connect with your true values
- create momentum
- find flow
- self-edit – what you say to yourself matters

I'll also introduce you to new systems and processes that will allow you to pursue your goals in a sustainable, healthy way, challenge outdated architecture that stands in the way of our ambitions, connect meaningfully and deeply with our own world view, find compassion, for ourselves and others, break down barriers, define what having it all really means, and how we can achieve it. I am proof that in order to achieve long- term success, you do not need to cut out hobbies, people, places and things that bring you fulfilment. Instead, you need smarter systems and processes in order to enable you to do it all.

Why *Women*?

Women are supposed to be absolute in our opinions, but not *forceful*. Directive but not *un-feminine*. Self-aware but not *self-assured*. Supportive but not *indulgent*. Naturally slim but not *too slim*. Sexy but not *slutty*. Successful but not *show-offs*. Mothers but not in the *workplace*. CEOs but not *boss bitches*. We're supposed to save money but also give to *causes*. To put ourselves first but not be *selfish*. To be fashionable but not *dress for the male gaze*. To outperform our competition but not by *too much*. To make money but *be humble*. To take but give back. To be feminists, but without alienating men. To discuss our bodies but without being crude. To be fun but not *irresponsible*.

Everywhere you look, it seems that hypocrisy is the cornerstone of modern feminism. No wonder we are all so exhausted. We have previously viewed and understood burnout and work-related stress through the male lens. This means that there are less than adequate solutions for – and a total lack of understanding about – how women can overcome the paralysing effects of burnout.

The truth is, men don't have to prove they 'deserve' their place at the table as much as women do.

A number of times in my career, I have experienced shock and apathy from men when they are faced with women in leadership roles. I was once told point-blank by a man in his sixties, a previous CEO of a US pharmaceutical company, that he would respect me more if I was a man. I have been asked how much money my father gave me to start my company. While there are men who are good at their jobs, there are also many more women who are overlooked, diminished and gaslit (thrilled I've got that word in this early on), and who have to work harder and harder to get their equal share.

According to a study conducted by McKinsey, burnout is hitting women in leadership the hardest, with at least fifty per cent saying they are experiencing burnout at work. In 2020 alone, a quarter of females in senior leadership positions said they were ready to downshift their careers or leave the workforce. Today, the number of women looking to offload major roles or quit has increased to one in every three senior-level women.

It's a hugely complex task trying to fight this archaic system while simultaneously subscribing to it in order to be successful. If we want to stay put, we have to do it through gritted teeth, enormous sacrifices, acting like a man, and considering second place the greatest achievement.

As we jostle for position, we also have to balance work, family life, fertility, misogyny and mental health – it's no wonder we find ourselves drained. We have been told that working hard, running ourselves into the ground, working late, over-caffeinating, sleeping four hours a night (thank you, Thatcher), being the first in and last out, sacrificing our personal lives, and eating on the go, are all conducive to succeeding in the long term. But instead, women are burned out.

That's why I'm here. The Smarter Method will encourage you to prioritise yourself in order to work smarter and stop pouring your energy into bottomless sources such as unfulfilling work or dreaded social plans. Instead, you will learn how to channel it into meaningful pursuits. It will help you to reframe the idea of over-productivity equalling advancement. And ultimately, it will teach you that those who work smarter are those who achieve more long-term success.

I'm here to tell you that our archaic tropes of business success are inconsistent with the modern structures that provide balance.

THE 10 Ms

I have structured this book around the ten lessons that have helped me the most. These are lessons that I have learned personally, or that have been shared with me by some of the most impressive people I have worked with. In an age of information fatigue, I have created a straightforward set of steps that are easy to integrate into your life and work. This book holds over a decade of real-life, practical learning on the job, and is designed to help you live a less-stressed life.

Each chapter starts with the key themes, so it's super easy to return to time and time again when you need a reminder. There's no expectation that you will do all of this at the same time. The Smarter Method encourages you to iterate, flex and move with what works for you, mastering simple principles and reframing what you already know. Each chapter is themed around a helpful 'M', full of tips and tricks, explanations of why we defer to what we know, challenges to your current thinking, prompts, exercises, visuals, learnings, and lessons.

The benefits you can expect to see from this book are as follows:

- **Increased productivity** – When you work efficiently, you increase your overall productivity. You can complete more tasks in the same amount of time. You won't have to remove passions from your life in order to fit them all in.
- **Improved work–life balance** – If you can understand what this balance means for you, you can allocate more energy to a range of activities, including dating, spending time with friends and family, travelling, or trying out a new side hustle.
- **A new approach to challenges** – You can apply yourself to challenging tasks more effectively if you have more time and energy. Reframing new challenges as achievable rather than intimidating will help change the way you confront them.
- **Increased positivity** – Embracing the reality of living and working smarter will help you approach situations with an abundant mindset, helping you to get more done and feel great about it.

The Smarter Method is not about unlearning what you've been taught, it's about modifying what you already know.

I hope that as you read this book, you will learn, challenge, refine and implement the smarter systems and processes that enable you to live your life fully, however that looks for you. I wrote this book because I believe passionately that people can do incredible things. I've seen them. I resent viscerally the ideas that choosing a career means you aren't choosing motherhood, that choosing yourself means you aren't choosing others, or that choosing to follow a passion means you aren't following the system. Many of these things can coexist alongside each other. I have spent almost fifteen years exploring, getting it wrong, asking questions, absorbing, learning and ultimately thriving because of the systems in this book. I present to you a collection of all that I have learned about choosing to have it all. There is no suggestion that it's easy, but – I have to emphasise this – it is *possible*. I ask that you read this book with the belief that life can be big and full and exciting and abundant. My wish is that by the time you have finished reading, you will feel better armed to embrace that existence.

CHAPTER 1

Mornings

'Morning is an important time of day, because how you spend your morning can often tell you what kind of day you are going to have.'

LEMONY SNICKET

The morning is arguably the most important time of the day. Carpe the diem and all that shite. Outdated ideas about sticking with the mood you wake up with, waking up on the wrong side of bed, and needing multiple coffees before you function can be overwhelmingly negative. In this chapter, you will learn how to challenge the way things are, replacing them with smarter systems and processes that work for you and set you up for the day ahead. You'll consider why reducing the number of decisions you make in a day leads to greater efficiency, and how to identify whether a decision is even yours to make. I'll explain why waking up at the right time for you, and nobody else, is the key to a smarter day. I'll introduce you to the ten-second test, encouraging you to batch tasks and eliminate smaller jobs as soon as possible. The chapter will frame how to make your day work for you, and will provide you with essential tools so that you can start as you mean to go on.

SHOWING UP DAILY

WHAT IT ACTUALLY MEANS

Much of my working life has been dominated by an aggressive commitment to achieve. My perception of showing up was to arrive always at a ten out of ten. It has taken me a long time to reframe the idea of showing up. I've fought hard against the undulations that are natural day to day. The decisions we make in the morning shape our entire day. They are often based on the focus to achieve as much as possible, rather than to consider how we feel, what our state of mind is, how much natural energy we have, and whether we are experiencing burnout. Much of this chapter will encourage you to reconnect with yourself – figuring out what works for you, rather than borrowing others' definitions of what a successful day might look like. It is really important to be mindful of how you move through the day, and adjust accordingly based on a series of environmental factors, including sleep, mental agility, volume of tasks and whether or not you are operating in a burned-out state. Nailing your morning is a powerful way to direct the rest of your day.

First, let's do a temperature check of how you are feeling. Many of us can oscillate between extremes, with high cortisol and high anxiety, unable to take a breath and really understand what we are working with. The quiz below will help you identify whether or not you are in fact operating in a state of burnout.

The *Burnout* Quiz

Do you find that you never want to have sex, with yourself or anyone else?

Perhaps sex is the last thing on your mind, or feels like just another thing you have to do. A lack of libido and omission of any desire is a key symptom of burnout.

Do you literally have no fucks to give?

This type of apathy is consistent with burnout.

Do you never feel like socialising? Do you struggle to know what to have for breakfast, or what to wear?

Being burned out from decision fatigue means we struggle to care enough to make any sort of decision that could lead to dramatic changes, e.g. moving abroad or suddenly quitting your job.

Have you recently been a total raging bitch for no good reason?

This is a good indication that you are facing burnout. You have no tolerance left in you for anything, and your actions are based on panic and adrenaline instead of logic and analysis. This is often a way of counterbalancing the numbness you may feel – you need more extreme actions in order to generate stimulation, which can then lead to reckless or out-of-character behaviour.

Would you say generally you are tired?

If you constantly feel tired, no matter how much sleep you have had, and if your body aches, you have headaches, general fatigue, and a sense of feeling heavy all over, this is a good sign that your body isn't firing on all cylinders.

Do you often panic and obsessively worry about small things that you may or may not have done?

A constant underlying feeling of stress or anxiety isn't a state that you need to live in. It becomes all-consuming, destructive and exhausting, and you end up not being able to see the wood for the trees. Nausea, poor sleep, tears and loss of appetite are all symptoms of ongoing worry and anxiety.

BURNOUT

Sorry to tell you this, but if you answered 'yes' to more than two of the questions above, you may well have burnout. Burnout makes mornings impossible.

So, what are you going to do about it? Keep going until you drop? Stop altogether? Post your score on TikTok? Sure, all these things make sense in the short term, but let's talk about smarter, longer-term ways to handle the world in which we live. We don't have to oscillate between extremes. In this book, I hope to share with you what I have learned from over a decade of experiencing burnout, to save you tens of thousands of pounds by outlining the good (and bad!) solutions I have invested in, and to provide you with something that resembles hope. A light that shows you that it doesn't have to be that hard. That we all have more choice about the outcomes than we are led to believe. You are strong and brave and capable. Accepting yourself is critical to success; it's how you will be able to embrace your ability to excel without extinguishing your light.

One of the most important ways to identify and avoid burnout is to be clear about the trends and patterns that exist in your routine. In the same way that keeping a food diary provides an honest and sobering insight into our eating habits, the same methodology works for other habits. Given that habits are defined as behaviour that is repeated regularly and tends to occur subconsciously, this is an important place to start. You must commit to gaining clarity on what your habits are now, so that you can be in a more informed state of mind when it comes to positively influencing them.

Try using this simple template and begin by writing down habits as they come up in the day, with the time at which they happen.

Habit	*Time* Time of day you perform it

If you are struggling to identify habits, you can start with some of the below:

- drink water
- online shopping
- client work
- reply to group chat messages
- browse social media
- procrastinate
- exercise
- meditate
- listen to a podcast
- eat lunch

The reason for filling in this tracker is so that you can bring awareness to the automatic actions that you perform each day. If you are looking to make changes to your habits, identifying what they are and when they happen is an important step.

Tip: stick to fewer than ten habits, so you aren't overwhelmed.

Having sprinted on the circular burnout treadmill several times in my life, I can tell you a few things about careering head first into a brick wall. When I was twenty-four, HMRC bailiffs turned up at my office due to an unpaid tax bill of £60,000. After getting over the initial flattery that they thought I had anything of value in the office to take, I was made aware that my accountant had spent the VAT I had been saving. This meant that I entered into a one-year repayment plan with HMRC, repaying £5,000 per month. That was almost the entirety of my profit, and so I had to work extra hard just to stand still. I had no tools, understanding, literature or medication to help me understand or manage the stress that was related to my work at that time. I would have regular panic attacks, and a profound guilt around the fear of being found out. I ended up in hospital with a stomach ulcer, and remember trying to join a Zoom call while I was there. It was with a pet food brand, and I'd hazard a guess that they literally did not care whether I joined or not. At the time, it felt like the biggest meeting of my life.

Then came the Covid-19 pandemic, which was burnout central. The days were endless. The volume of information we had to wade through was extreme. Team issues ramped up, and I personally didn't have a proficient structure for remote working, or a robust HR department to respond to the increase in mental health variations. I would panic every single time my phone rang. I worked constantly because the alternative was difficult to face, and I worked the hardest I've ever worked to make the least money I've ever made. None of the advice, feedback or expert insights I sought out at this time spoke to me. They all felt like band-aid solutions spouted by people whose stress levels were piqued when their favourite candle was discontinued. So no, Sarah, a bath before bed won't help me get a good night's sleep. And no, Simon, lavender tea is not going to help when my anxiety is more ambitious than I am. Actually fuck off.

RESPECT YOUR NATURAL RHYTHMS

If I had a pound for every time I've lied about getting up early, I would be rich beyond my wildest dreams. Throughout my career, being an early riser was repeatedly framed as the key to success, and so it was a club I wanted to be part of. Or rather, a club I wanted people to think I was part of.

I remember doing an interview for a magazine about my daily routine, and feeling conflicted about whether to lie about the time I set my alarm to wake me up. I met in the middle and said I woke up at 7am. I absolutely do not wake up at 7am. I chose to lie. The reason for the lie seemed straightforward. Clients, team members and anyone else reading the article needed to think that I was a superpower in the making. That I had my shit together. That I rose at the crack of dawn to an alarm of applause, with a headset by my bed, ready to hop on a global call. At that time, I was highly affected by what I thought success was. I assumed that you needed to be more tired than anyone else, but also that you needed to have stacks of energy. That you awoke each morning because the burning power of your ideas was singeing through the pillow. That a morning coffee was slurped as you moved around to dress in the same outfit as the day before, because Steve Jobs did that and he's successful. I was playing business, and I was influenced entirely by the false narrative to which I had unknowingly subscribed.

So there we are: I lied. I regurgitated the lie that had been told to me and kept it rolling to other women. I am sorry.

I wake up at 8am. That is the truth.

It is with great pleasure that I tell you that getting up earlier doesn't actually make you more productive. I'd like to formally introduce the 8am club, a club to which I have subscribed for the last five years, and one which makes me entirely more productive.

Waking up early had the following effects on me:

- I worried the night before that I wouldn't get enough sleep.
- I felt like a personal failure when I inevitably hit snooze.
- I lied to people about my routine.
- I felt ashamed for lying (and ashamed that I felt like I needed to lie).
- I craved sugar and caffeine during the day.
- I was exhausted by early afternoon.
- I skipped gym sessions due to fatigue.
- I cancelled plans.

There was literally nothing positive for me in the 5am club, and yet I was willing, at great personal expense, to be part of a routine that didn't work for me, because of the status it offered and the shame I would feel if I wasn't included. My issue wasn't that I was trying to get up at 5am; my issue was that I was trying to live by a rhythm that wasn't natural for me.

Now here are the personal effects I've experienced as a member of the 8am club:

- I wake up feeling better rested.
- I enjoy a more relaxed morning routine.
- I feel more present for my morning in the office.
- I am more likely to make better decisions relating to sugar, caffeine and food.
- I feel less sluggish after lunch.
- I rarely miss an evening gym session.
- I feel more in control of my energy and routine.
- I feel proud that I am showing up for myself and my rhythm.

There are quite literally thousands of studies and books exploring sleep and how it supercharges all human activity. But whether it's 8am, 7am or 9am, the only right time to rise is the one that works for you. The main takeaway should be that you need to have restful, balanced sleep – ideally, eight hours' worth (cue eye roll from the parents reading this book). A 2017 Harvard study found that it doesn't matter whether you sleep early and wake up early or vice versa.[1] The most important thing is that you're consistent about your schedule.

From personal experience, no one thing can unlock transformation on its own, but making small steps that relate to meaningful change sets you off on the path towards a more controlled, balanced approach to your wellbeing. Taking charge of structures that work best for you as you start the day is hugely empowering and leads to long-term success. When it comes to sleep and waking up, it's all about understanding your circadian rhythm.

WTF Is My *Circadian Rhythm?*

That's a great question. And another great question is: how the fuck do I pronounce this word? Circadian is pronounced 'sir-kay-dee-un'. And according to the Sleep Foundation, here's what it means:

> [Over] millions of years, life has been shaped by the world's rhythmic shifts of night and day. Many living things – including plants, animals, and humans – have circadian rhythms, which are tailored to life on earth and the changes that occur as the planet rotates on its axis. Every 24 hours, predictable shifts in light and temperature take place. Circadian rhythms help living things respond to changes in their environment.
>
> In humans, circadian rhythms serve many functions, including helping regulate:
>
> - sleeping and waking
> - core body temperature
> - the immune system
> - hormones
> - metabolism
> - cognitive function
> - the body's reaction to stress[2]

If you feel sluggish in the morning or need a mid-afternoon nap, or if you're feeling jet-lagged when all you've done is walk to the office, it may be that you've disrupted your circadian rhythm. When I think of mine, I think of it as a biological clock. Sometimes that clock runs perfectly; at other times, it needs a service. A lack of sleep regulation is the easiest way to send this 'tick' out of whack, and understanding your sleep needs is the easiest and most efficient way to get it working well again. Being in touch with your own rhythm, and understanding when and how to service it, will enable you to make better, more informed decisions about what you need in order to reduce stress and become more productive.

In addition to feeling tired, for many of us, it's the extra pressure of the shame that comes with tiredness, or convincing ourselves we are unproductive. It's helpful to refer to the graphic on page 12, and consider what you feel showing up every day looks like. There is no expectation that you operate at a ten every single day. Life is long (hopefully), and it is the management and maintenance of your time in the long term that will help you achieve success.

Wake up at a time that works with your circadian rhythm (as long as it doesn't make you late for work!). Listen to yourself, not the nonsense of the world, and pay attention to your tiredness. If you have had a hard, gruelling week, for the love of God sleep in on Saturday or budge your alarm to an hour later on Friday. Be kind to the best tool you have at your disposal: yourself.

REPLICATE REALISTIC ROUTINES

At the start of my health and fitness journey, I would spend hours looking at images on social media of women with a wide range of body types. I compared myself endlessly to these women, and I was setting myself up to fail by making comparisons to completely unrealistic goals. On one particular day, I moaned to my personal trainer that it was impossible to look like the female PTs in the gym. He told me plainly that of course it was, 'You come to the gym for three hours a week, they are here eight hours a day, and only eat chicken breast and rice.' His point was clear – you cannot expect to mimic the results of others when you're putting in way less of the work.

In my approach to the mornings, I was tormented by the Mark Wahlberg morning routine. Waking up at 3 am, reading three books before breakfast, completing an online course, whipping up a meal for all the family, two conference calls, an hour and a half of meditation followed by two hours in the gym. And THEN he starts his day. The thing about this, which I cannot stress enough, is that your morning IS a part of your day. You're not supposed to do a day before you start the day. You aren't expected to replicate the results of someone operating in a completely different environment either. Don't ignore the fact that it's easier to accomplish all of these things if you're lucky enough to have a gym in your basement, an in-house chef, a PA to arrange your day. Look for tips and tricks from those who are living their life in a way that feels possible for you. Set yourself up to win.

WAKE UP AND WIN

'The first hour is the rudder of the day.'

Henry Ward Beecher

I cannot over-emphasise the power of achieving something small for yourself first thing in the morning. A common symptom of burnout is a lack of motivation. I remember waking up after a night of broken sleep, feeling anxious about the day ahead, and looking for reasons to reaffirm why I was useless. I'd usually eat a biscuit or nibble on something that I thought I shouldn't be eating, thus resigning myself to the fact that I'd already ruined the day. As I began to master the skills of a smarter morning, I understood the importance of accomplishing something at the start of the day. I tried big things first, ambitious as I was. I booked 6 am spinning classes, or prepped for a mid-December early morning run (I even bought a head torch . . .). Needless to say, I failed to commit to any of these, as again I was copying the routine of someone who was setting unrealistic expectations for me. If going to the gym in the morning or building a Lego house before 7am brings you joy, by all means go for it. But for many of us, it's easier to start small. Make the bed, complete Wordle, do a crossword, water your plants, read a page of your (this) book or tidy the bathroom. These smaller tasks can be reframed as moments to win, setting you on a more productive course for the rest of the morning.

Remove *Morning Decisions* by Doing Them the Night Before

Any form of decision-making takes up energy. Every time you engage your brain to make a decision, you're using mental energy. If you're stacking your mornings with a bunch of huge decisions, you'll likely be feeling flat before you've even arrived at your first task of the day. The key to energy preservation with regards to your mornings is twofold:

1. Preparation = Consistency
2. Repetition = Automation

Preparation and repetition

If meal prepping feels like a toxic phrase to you, don't do it. But you can decide what you're going to eat, even if you don't have the desire to actually prep the meal. I eat a variation of three things for breakfast, every single day. I don't prep them, I just know what they are. I don't even think about it. I automatically choose one of those three things. This means that I don't waste any energy on that decision in the morning.

The same goes for choosing an outfit. Have you ever woken up in a good mood, only to try on four different outfits, fail to find the shoes you want to wear and realise that your favourite underwear is still in the wash? That alone is enough to turn your good mood into a bad one. David Beckham has a rail with all of his outfits for the week. David Beckham also has a walk-in closet and a personal stylist. I have a DIY rail from Argos. It does the trick. On a Sunday, I look at my diary for the week, to see if there is anything specific that I will need to wear. For events in public relations, we generally wear black. If I've booked workouts, I'll know how many sets of leggings and sports bras I'll need. While I don't plan the entire week in one go, I certainly plan for the next day. This means that I remove any friction in the process, making it seamless, fast and enjoyable.

In addition to food and clothing, prep can extend to your journey to work. I have two travel options in terms of audio. *Harry Potter*, or the *Smarter* playlist on Audible. I assume you'll have three given you'll be listening to this book . . .

Audio can impact mood regulation. I imagine you've felt the power of a great tune, and similarly, listening to Snow Patrol for hours on end can make you feel quite down. Planning your playlist for the morning means that you are setting an intention for your mood. You're reducing decision-making and any issues for your commute. If content is downloaded, you won't need to be online to access it, so no buffering on the tube, and no mindless scrolling on apps you don't need to be on that early.

In addition to audio, a remarkably impactful piece of prep is Google Street View. If ever I have a meeting in a new location, am attending a new fitness studio I haven't been to, or am venturing into the unknown, I always review the route the night before, using Street View to highlight precisely what the building looks like. Living and working in London means that I have regularly attended meetings in confusing locations, found it difficult to find the right entrance, or underestimated the time between arrival, and getting to the right floor. Years ago,

I arrived fifteen minutes early to a client meeting the before realising I was in the WeWork opposite the WeWork they were located in, making me late. Being prepared, on time and calm on arrival gives you more time and energy to focus on what is actually important. As you repeat the systems that work best for you, they will become second nature, thus helping to shape a more productive morning routine.

Don't Hit *Snooze*

It's tempting to press snooze on your alarm when you wake up unmotivated for the day ahead and don't feel fully rested from the night before. If you are in the throes of burnout, dragging yourself out of bed in the morning can feel like climbing Everest, particularly if you are trying to get up at a time that isn't aligned with your own rhythm. When your alarm goes off in the morning, you wake up (stay tuned for more huge scientific revelations). When you hit snooze, you start to drift off again, which triggers another sleep cycle that can last between seventy-five and ninety minutes. If you're snoozing for ten minutes, you are disrupting your new sleep cycle so it's no wonder that you wake up feeling groggy. Hitting snooze creates a state of sleep inertia and it can take up to four hours to shake that feeling.

Opt for *Airplane Mode*

I have been most undisciplined with my phone when I am in bed. The doom scroll is real. When I embarked on my smarter journey, I found it difficult to understand how to practise good phone discipline in the morning. My alarm was on my phone, the thunderstorm playlist was on my phone, I'd have to check my emails first thing in case any meetings changed or if there was something I needed to know before I went into the office. I ended up falling asleep with my phone surgically attached to my hand. I'd check TikTok, emails, Slack, the news, my Monday app, Instagram and LinkedIn just in case there were any major business updates, all before 9am . . .

Our relationship with our phone is complex and breaking the bad habits is tricky, especially in the mornings. Exposing yourself to mindless screentime the moment you wake up is nothing other than a terrible way to start the day. It requires discipline to stop, but reducing phone time in the AM has some tangible benefits. Here are some helpful tips:

- Switch your phone light from blue to orange. Orange light doesn't affect your eyes as much, can reduce tension headaches, and doesn't disrupt your circadian rhythm.
- Turn off your phone notifications. There's nothing more panic-inducing than waking up to a bunch of messages that are not urgent but feel urgent because they are staring you in the face.
- Choose home apps. This is something that transformed my mornings. I don't look at social media apps when I am at home. It limits mood-altering content as you start your day.

- Don't use your phone alarm. I bought an alarm clock, so that I wouldn't need to rely on my phone to wake me up in the morning.
- Get a speaker. Anything I listen to for sleep is played through a speaker, which means I don't need my phone near me to play it.
- The first time I look at emails is when I am at my desk. I used to read my emails in the morning, and with international clients, the difference in time zones meant that emails from the night before would throw me off course before I'd even got out of bed. Now, I only read my emails when I'm at my desk, laptop or computer. I realised that if I had a stressful email waiting for me, I could protect my peace on my commute, and deal with it post-coffee, when I was in the right environment, rather than letting it derail me first thing.
- Put your phone out of reach. In the morning I'd automatically reach for my phone – it was usually next to my hand or in my bed. I now leave it on the other side of the room, and instead have water, my vitamins, face cream, my alarm clock and a book within arm's reach instead.
- Switch to aeroplane mode. If you want to activate beast mode, the best thing you can do is switch to aeroplane mode, and not switch back until you're in the office or at your desk. This is hardcore, but if you download the podcasts and audio you want to listen

to on your commute and plan your journey in advance, then it is possible. This means you can ensure that your morning routine is focused on setting you up for the day ahead.

TRACK ENERGY, NOT TIME

The idea of time-management being the elixir of productivity has been drummed into us – HR modules are shaped around how to manage our time, personal work objectives detail whether we are or aren't good at managing our time, and lateness suggests we have no respect for the person we are meeting. The problem with trying to manage time is that it's basically impossible, because it's a moving target. Many of us waste important energy in the morning on tasks, distractions and jobs that we don't need to. Being connected to your energy is at the heart of the Smarter Method.

On the surface, it shouldn't be overcomplicated – we literally have the same number of hours every single day. Many people construct their working day based on an eight-hour day – let's assume one that runs from 9am to 5pm. When it comes to managing that time, the usual approach is: 'How can I get as much done as possible before 5pm rolls around?' We fly out of the blocks at 9am, sit at our desk, fuelled by coffee and anxiety for the day ahead, and from then on, it's a race against the clock. It's very easy to see how that ingrained attitude leads quickly, and directly, to burnout. What time-management doesn't take into consideration are the ebbs and flows of our energy, our hormones, and our overall capacity, and how they vary each day.

While we do have to acknowledge and appreciate time each day from an organisational perspective, making a switch to focusing on managing my energy, not my time, was profoundly beneficial. In this context, 'energy' is the strength and vitality required for sustained physical or mental activity.

We typically focus more on the number of tasks we can fit into the time available, rather than the amount of energy we have to deliver those tasks. We need to match our energy to a task in order to excel.

I believe our energy levels fall into four main categories:

- **Silence** – Your energy is so depleted that you flick into silent mode.
- **Hum** – You're ticking along, but it's relatively low vibe.
- **Sing** – You're listening to the office conversation, but not fully getting involved. If asked, you could give a great answer.
- **Shout** – You're bouncing off the walls.

This is useful because it allows you to make an assessment of your energy levels and bring some awareness to what you are working with for the day ahead. If your morning vibe is a Hum, it makes more sense to ensure you are reducing taxing tasks early on in the day. It's helpful to identify patterns and consider how your routine impacts your energy levels. Note: you cannot operate at a Shout for the entire day. You will fluctuate.

A *Useful* Exercise

Spend one working week tracking your energy in relation to the tasks you hope to complete. Ask yourself:

- When do I feel most sluggish?
- When do I have the most natural energy?
- When do I feel most creative?
- When do I feel most sensitive?
- When do I find it easier to concentrate?
- When am I most hungry?
- When do I feel invincible?

After reviewing your answers to these questions, you can now identify a more constructive overview of your capacity on a daily basis – and this in turn can show you when to perform the important tasks.

If you have a big project due this week, when is it best for you to do it? You might be tempted to start it on Monday at 9am because you are just so stressed about it, or you might leave it until Friday at 9am because you have been putting it off out of fear of how much of your day it will take up. I doubt either of these is actually the best time for the task. That will probably be something rather innocuous, like Wednesday at 10.30am. Perhaps that is your golden time each week, when you are best placed to do the best work in the most efficient way. Identify this time and use this knowledge to your advantage. Later, I will talk about time-blocking, which can help set structures and consistency around these times (see page 87).

Urgent *or* Important?

When you're headed towards burnout, it can feel impossible to differentiate between what is urgent and what is important. 'Urgent' here is defined as a task that requires attention given its imminent deadline. Depending on what job you are doing, this attention might be needed immediately, or within an hour. 'Important', meanwhile, is a task that is still meaningful, but not attached to a short time frame or deadline.

In a state of burnout, most of us find it difficult to work out the difference. *Everything* feels urgent. As such, you can end up moving from one task to another at rapid speed, making simple mistakes, feeling like a failure because of said mistakes, and then repeating the cycle. It's therefore really challenging to ever feel as though you are making progress, and you start to self-label as someone disorganised and unthorough. On page 146, we'll look more closely at how to establish whether a task is urgent or important.

Our energy has four dimensions: the body, emotions, mind and spirit. In an ideal world, these would be balanced all the time, with each source accounting for twenty-five per cent of our energy. Many of us consider this to be true balance, true equilibrium.

However, we don't live in a perfect world, so you can forget an even split. If you are depleting much more of your physical energy, you have to alter the other segments in order to use the stores you have.

Energy is finite, which means that you have to manage it accordingly. If you have a more emotionally exhausting week coming up, you will have to make thoughtful adjustments, such as reducing intense physical workouts, opting instead for something more gentle. Balance doesn't have to mean the scales are equal, it means that you have to iterate and make adjustments based on an understanding of where your energy is required. Decide which of the four dimensions is the priority.

The energy we give to tasks that are connected to each of these areas determines what stores we have left at the end of the day. For example, if you are working really hard for a promotion, you might be using much more energy for your mind and emotions. Learning how to regulate and renew your energy by making tasks automatic, unconscious or habitual allows us to establish systems that better direct our energy. Once you understand these cycles, you can better allocate a power hour, and identify your biological prime time.

Biological prime time – author Sam Carpenter coined this term in his book *Work the System,* 'this is when focus comes easier'.

Power hour – a power hour is a considered a one-hour length of time in which you can access your flow. This means fewer, if any, distractions, combined with elevated energy stores, hyper focus and commitment to a specific task.

> 'The ultimate measure of our lives is
> not how much time we spend on the
> planet, but rather how much energy
> we invest in the time we have.'
>
> *Jim Loehr*

The benefits of tracking your energy are that you can then choose how you direct your time. Energy informs time.

World-renowned performance psychologist Dr Jim Loehr has some really interesting thoughts on our energy and how when we are accessing our best energy, it flows from the perception of opportunity, adventure and challenge. He discusses that we need to focus on the *quality* of our energy. This is why it's important to consider Silence, Hum, Sing, Shout. We need to be connected to our deeply held values, have a realistic optimism for the work at hand, experience positive emotions and ensure our sleep habits are paramount.

Let's return to the some of the questions on page 34. Here are some examples of how you can use your answers to these questions to work out how to be smarter with the energy reserves that you have by directing your time accordingly.

When do I feel most sluggish?

If sluggishness hits you after lunch, this could be because of what you are eating or drinking. However, we do have natural cycles throughout the day, and you can't be 'on' for eight hours or more. Once you've identified the times that you feel sluggish, look to allocate low-effort tasks. Alternatively, change your scenery. Get offsite for a walk, exercise or listen to a podcast. In the morning, you can better inform this by optimising your routine and commute.

When do I have the most natural energy?

For me, this is from mid-morning until about 3pm. I prefer to be at my desk at this time, working on tasks that require more energy, such as writing decks, forward planning or assessing financial documents.

When do I feel most creative?

This is the sort of energy that feeds your soul. Creative energy is precious and needs a safe space to be directed in a positive way. Trying to complete creative tasks when we feel sluggish or have low energy levels removes any joy from them. In addition, it's difficult to fully exercise your creative brain when your energy levels are low. As such, identify when you feel most creative. There are two times of day for me when this happens: usually around mid-afternoon, and then at some point in the night. As a result, I have a small ideas notepad by my bed, in which I scribble the thoughts that inconveniently wake me up. Some of the best ideas I have ever had have been captured in my little bedside book.

DECISION-MAKING

In an interview with David Rubenstein, Amazon founder, Jeff Bezos, explained that he feels the need to only make three good decisions a day.[3] (He doesn't specify how many *bad* decisions he makes on a daily basis, but we can assume it is not a high number.) It is estimated that adults make on average around 35,000 remotely conscious decisions each day.[4] Remotely conscious decisions include things such as deciding to sip from a glass of water or talk in a meeting. All those decisions require an engagement of cognitive function; in other words, they mean we need to use our brains. This all accumulates – quite literally, the decisions add up in our heads – and it can mean that our ability to make good decisions can be eroded. This can lead to decision fatigue, 'the deteriorating quality of decisions made by an individual after a long session of decision-making'.[5] Essentially, it means that we make shitty decisions. When we're in a state of decision fatigue, we tend to look for shortcuts and resort to suboptimal strategies. We may avoid the decision altogether by procrastinating, or we may swing to the other extreme and make an impulsive choice.[6] If we are repeatedly giving time and energy to these decisions, they will reduce our energy. Creating automation with these decisions, usually as a result of a considered routine that is thoughtful about your biological prime time, will ensure you use less energy to make the decision, and reduce, or avoid entirely, poor decision-making.

Have you ever reached a restaurant in the evening and found yourself completely nonplussed about what to order? Are you ever unable to decide whether to get a cab or the tube? Or unsure of what to wear? This level of indecision doesn't come from being a person who finds it hard to make decisions. It comes from the fact that you've used up all your decision-making juice for the day, and thus find yourself apathetic. In addition to the remotely conscious decisions I mentioned earlier, research commissioned by psychology-based app Noom found that adults make an average of 122 informed choices every day – but that doesn't mean the decision is final. A staggering eighty-seven per cent of those polled admitted to changing their minds.[7]

There are three stages to good, effective decision-making: the three Cs.

- **Clarify** – Clearly identify the decision to be made or the problem to be solved.
- **Consider** – Think about the possible choices and what would happen for each choice. Think about the potential positive and negative consequences of each choice.
- **Choose** – Make a decision and choose to action it.

It is also important to choose which decisions matter. Those that matter tend to be confined to problem-solving. For example, if decisions become habits, they become remotely conscious. A remotely conscious decision is automatic and uses very little energy. Leaving to go to the gym to make a 7 pm gym class isn't a decision if it's diarised and part of your routine. It takes very little cognitive function to action that commitment. This is why Steve Jobs wore the same clothes every day. Disorganised people will often tell you they are the most busy and drained. They use their time incredibly inefficiently, largely due to poor planning. As such, each decision has to be made under pressure, using multiple dimensions of energy sources. Very few decisions for these individuals are automatic because of a lack of routine, leading to an underwhelming output from the perceived amount of work happening. This in turn leads to unreliability, a hectic energy, fatigue, lack of rest and, overall, unproductivity.

You can integrate your 'three good decisions' into your energy-tracking for the day – your good decisions are best made when you feel creative, tolerant and full of energy (ideally your power hour or your biological prime time). For Jeff

Bezos, the three good decisions relate to choices that only he can make. As the CEO of a multi-billion-dollar company, the mental energy and impact of those decisions is so significant that up to three of them will suffice. Before you solve a problem, it is also important that you identify whether it is your problem to solve. The Smarter Method asks you to consider your energy stores throughout the day. Allocating energy to making decisions that don't require your input is a complete waste of your time (and energy). Many people facing burnout struggle to take a moment to consider whether they need to be using their mental energy at all. It is difficult to have any critical distance when you are in, or heading for, a state of burnout, and so your ability to decide on where to attribute your energy is reduced. In extreme cases, this can lead to decision paralysis. We'll explore this more in the section on delegation (page 150).

How Do I Know If It's *My Decision* to Make?

- Is there anyone else who could make the decision? If so, let them. Delegation is an important skill to master to be an effective decision-maker.
- What is the likely outcome with the information that you have?
- What is your gut telling you?
- Why do I want to make this decision? Is it because no one else has the answer, or because I want people to know I can make the decision?

- Check in with your energy dimensions – am I able to make this decision based on how I am feeling?

When you're using the Smarter Method, you aren't being asked to learn hundreds of new systems and processes. You are being asked to apply what you know to existing problem areas, in scenarios that work well for you. Understanding whether something is 'your problem' – and getting comfortable with the idea that it might, in fact, not be – is a crucial part of ensuring the method works well for you.

Decision-Making Tips

- **End the thought.** The mornings can be overwhelming due to the number of potential decisions, tasks, meetings and problems to solve. Don't allow thoughts to become tributaries that just continuously flow. You have to learn how to end the thought, complete it, and move on to the next one. The best way to do this is to write down the actual, singular issue that you are facing. Draw a circle round it and let it live as one problem. Simplifying your thought process will make coming to a decision easier. The best way to use these circles is for larger, more important decisions, rather than for tiny tasks.

- **Don't conflate the issues.** We've all allowed ourselves to run away with a narrative that just because we've lost one client, all of them will leave. It's important that one issue doesn't become ten. One is easier to deal with than ten. If you squash ten issues into one circle, it will become squashed and chaotic. Ten separate circles that you can tick off one by one is far more manageable.
- **Resist speaking to yourself in extremes.** If you fall out with one person, it doesn't mean that all your friends hate you. If you don't get the job, it doesn't mean you are unemployable. Focus on the specific issue at present rather than the possibility of this becoming a blanket rule across everything you are doing.
- **Identify with the reaction you want to have.** What would a calm person do? What would a professional person do? Decide what type of person you want to be, and mimic how they would respond.
- **Make the decision.** Indecision is purgatory. Right or wrong, a decision made moves the story on. Smart people make decisions.

'It's important to be willing to make mistakes. The worst thing that can happen is you become memorable.'

Sara Blakely, founder of Spanx

MAKING A PRIORITY LIST

I have strong feelings about daily planners. I think they are a terrible accessory for anyone with a penchant for procrastination; they are like colouring-in books for untethered adults. I find that most people spend more time on their planners than they do on actually carrying out the tasks they write in them. If you're devoting time to decorating an elaborate diary, it usually means you're falling into the trap of productivity theatre.

What *is* useful is identifying and writing down your top-line tasks for the day, to offer clarity and help you to allocate your energy (and time) in the most productive way. Writing a simple priority list, such as the one below, keeps focus on the important decisions for the day.

Simple *Priority* List

- Review contract amendments for new client win, and return the document.
- Call X to give them feedback from previous line-management meeting.
- Review and sign off next month's social media plan.
- Draft press release for new client announcement.

OVERCOMING CHALLENGES

Throughout your working life, you will face a number of frustrating, inefficient, infuriating, unfair and challenging situations. The ability to consider these as isolated incidents is a skill, and you have much more control over them than you think, but all too often we simply blame these things on a 'bad day', which then sets us up for more frustration as we're anticipating that it will continue.

If your first thought upon waking up is about how stressful your day is going to be, you're essentially predetermining your reaction to it – regardless of whether or not what you're worried about even ends up happening. This is called anticipatory stress. Sometimes, the speed with which we jump into the day gives us very little time for a change of direction. If we start out already feeling stressed or in a bad mood, it means that we move into our day with a bad attitude. There is absolutely no reason for this to be our chosen mood for the day. It takes up too much energy and focus. It is not smart working.

Here are six easy ways to snap out of the morning grumps or overcome a challenge without letting it derail you.

1. **Try reframing** – Consider the position you are in from an alternative point of view. How would a positive person look at it? What would your best friend tell you to do?
2. **Challenge yourself** – Remind yourself that the mood

you have woken up with doesn't need to be the one you wear for the entire day.

3. **Remember you have much more control than you think.** You have the power to take actions that ensure your days work better for you. The day doesn't happen *to* you.
4. **Take a moment.** Before you jump into your first job of the day, take five minutes to reset. This could be a moment of silence, a meditation, a short walk, some breath work or whatever works for you.
5. **Try and identify the underlying reason you feel anxious, worried or stressed.** Can you address it directly, rather than allowing it to influence your entire day? This requires self-discipline and an awareness or connection to a deeper level of thought. We often find ourselves misdirecting our annoyance towards something totally unrelated.
6. **Accept that some days are difficult.** The ability to tolerate a bad day is a realistic and useful life skill. Not every day is going to be a fabulous day. Sometimes, you get bad news, things don't go your way and you feel like it's you against the world. And sometimes, you just need to ride out those days, do things that you like, keep disciplined, avoid mindless habits like scrolling on your phone, rest and reset so you're ready for the next day.

OVERCOMING PROCRASTINATION

The *Ten-Second* Test

The ten-second test is a useful tool to shape your productivity. I started using it to help me clear my monster inbox, but have found that it fits naturally into so many other parts of my life, and can boost productivity both in and outside of work.

The ten-second test relates to tiny tasks, those you can do in ten seconds or less. It helps you to avoid procrastination and reduce the headspace taken up by tiny tasks. The idea is simple: if you can check it off within ten seconds, do it straight away.

For example:

- adding something to your diary
- googling just about anything
- sending a Slack message
- replying to an email to confirm something
- setting up your timer (we'll talk about timers on page 85)
- emailing a Google document
- downloading a WeTransfer
- putting on your running shoes
- texting someone 'thank you'

We are so often wired to put things off, pushing important tasks aside because we think we can do them later. But those pushed-aside tasks can accumulate, until you're left with ninety flagged emails, countless unread WhatsApp messages, and a whole lotta stress. Think of it like taking the stairs rather than the lift. Although taking the stairs once is not enough to have an impact on your health, if you make a habit of it over time, it can make a real difference. Getting on with these tiny actions can help you feel more in control of your day, which reduces your stress levels and your workload.

Why Do We *Procrastinate*?

Procrastination is the act of delaying something or putting it off. It's RIFE in the morning. Here is a clever graph to demonstrate:

THE TEN-SECOND TEST

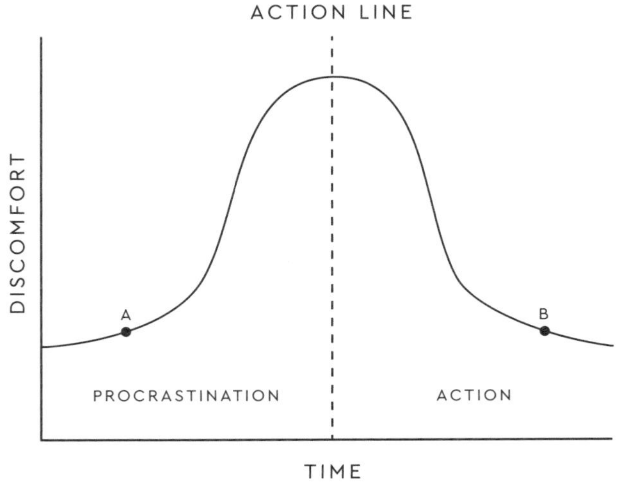

There are a number of reasons why we might procrastinate:

- We dread the task, and the unpleasantness associated with it makes us not want to do it. The dread often feels greater in the morning as we haven't yet begun the day.
- We doubt our ability to complete the task.
- We are unable to separate tasks - compounding them makes them difficult to address.
- We feel anxious or insecure.

Research shows that procrastination is linked to mood regulation. It's useful here to refer back to the idea of tracking your energy, not your time (see page 32). *When* you tackle a task has a huge impact on how (and if) it will be completed.

Types *of* Procrastinator

You know you are a procrastinator. You know because you have the ability to be incredibly efficient and find your flow with everything else other than the thing you actually need to do. At university, I used to tidy the cutlery drawer when I was supposed to be doing research for my dissertation. But there are four types of procrastinator – which one applies to you?

The performer

This is me. A performer forces themself to do work by leaving everything until the last minute. I used to justify this by saying,

'I work well under pressure,' while actually working terribly under pressure by burning out and feeling miserable.

Tip: Decide when you will start the task, rather than when you will finish it. You may even begin by seeing it as a tiny task.

The self-deprecator

This has also been me at times in my life. The 'I'm a worthless piece of shit who will never achieve anything' character. I'm sure she's familiar to you too. In this persona, you bully yourself into thinking that you've achieved nothing, and never will. Nothing is good enough and you confirm your own failure by avoiding doing the thing.

The over-booker

The 'I'm so busy' friend. Way too much in the diary, always busy, always talking about being busy. She never has enough time for anything – but what is she actually *doing*? She loves a long to-do list, which never gets done, and you couldn't possibly understand how much she has on.

The novelty-seeker

Have you ever experienced 'shiny object syndrome', the idea that there is always something sexier and more exciting to pursue? Are you unable to actually complete a task? Novelty-seekers have always just had 'the best idea' and have boundless energy for something new as soon as something current is more than an hour old.

This is all well and good – but what are you going to do about it?

Grow Up *and* Stop Procrastinating

- Throw away your daily planner. Gel pens are not a mark of status and you aren't going to win any competitions for writing out your to-do list nicely.
- Commit to the ten-second test – if you can do it in ten seconds, do it now.
- Track your energy, not your time (see page 32).
- Close your tabs. If you have to write a document, shut down your inbox, news app and Slack, so that you aren't distracted by a sexier prospect popping up on your screen.
- Use a desk timer. Set that baby up in twenty-minute increments so that you can time-block (we'll talk about this on page 87).
- Connect things you do want to do with things you don't want to do. I wanted to reduce my reality television habit (*Real Housewives* till I die), but instead of setting an unrealistic expectation, I decided I'd only watch it in the gym. I subsequently go to the gym far more than I used to.
- Be realistic about when you need to go all-in. Sometimes self-care isn't taking a bath. It's working late, ordering a pizza and getting the important thing done so that it's off your plate.

- Set yourself up to win. Your working environment has a profound impact on your ability to perform. Is a loud coffee shop with a door constantly opening and closing and people chatting a good environment for you? Do you need noise-cancelling headphones? (Pro tip: listen to a 'relaxing massage' playlist and thank me later.)
- Learn how to separate the urgent from the important (see page 146).

MAKE SOMEONE ELSE'S DAY

The simplest way to start your day smarter is to trigger feel-good messages in your brain. Doing good for others, often referred to as altruistic behaviour, can activate the brain's rewards circuitry. Put simply, doing good makes you feel good. Scientists have referred to this as a 'helper's high'. As you start your day, consider what you could do to make someone else's. The simplest ideas are:

- smiling on the tube
- buying a coffee for someone
- sending a voice note to a friend to check in
- complimenting a stranger on their outfit
- telling your colleague their hair looks great

- saying hello to a dog
- posting a card that you know the recipient will love receiving
- dropping off some clothes at your local charity shop

The most successful people prepare and plan for the day ahead, thus reducing the energy they have to use on decisions in the morning. Setting yourself up to win in the morning dictates your entire day, and it's integral to the Smarter Method.

CHAPTER 2

Message

'You can only become truly accomplished at something you love. Don't make money your goal. Instead, pursue the things you love doing and then do them so well that people can't take their eyes off of you.'

MAYA ANGELOU

None of us are suffering from a shortage of messages. Everywhere we look, new channels, content creators, advertisements, films, television shows, politicians, brands, strangers online and faceless voices on the radio and podcasts are bombarding us with information. Filtering these messages and cutting through the noise can, at times, feel like an impossible task. In this chapter, you'll look at how to cultivate an abundant mindset, how visualisation can become an incredibly powerful tool in helping you to move closer to your goals, why being 100 per cent sure about anything isn't the goal, and how to engage with and trust your gut. Each of us is individually responsible for creating the life that we want, and controlling the messages you receive and put out into the world is an integral part of living abundantly.

YOU HAVE TO SEE IT TO BELIEVE IT

Without doubt, the most powerful shift for me in both my career and my personal life came from letting go of my learned beliefs about what my life was going to look like. I hadn't believed that I could work with certain clients, wear certain clothes, look a certain way, earn a certain amount of money. I had resigned myself to a belief system that was at odds with my own ambitions. While I really wanted to do well in many aspects of my life, I hadn't yet understood how to fully own the vision of what I wanted to create myself.

Visualisation is an incredibly powerful tool. You quite literally have to see it to believe it. For many of us, our limiting beliefs prevent us from even believing in the possibility of the image. So it's not surprising that it's impossible to make that blurry image a reality. Much of the practice of manifesting, hypnotherapy, meditation and goal-setting centres around a version of visualisation. Repetitive cues – whether in our imagination, on our phone backgrounds, or roughly cut out and stuck on the wall – enable us to keep focused on a visual goal.

'I don't focus on what I'm up against. I focus on my goals and I try to ignore the rest.'

Venus Williams

There are two important things to note here. The first is that I had awareness of this technique, even if I wasn't yet able to successfully apply it. In my late twenties, I tried hypnotherapy, with great success. In this practice, in a state of deep relaxation, I was encouraged to see, on an imaginary cinema screen, the current vision of myself. I was then challenged to create, in the top left-hand corner of that screen, a square containing a much smaller image, this time of the person I wanted to be. This was always the same image for me. I was standing in a black tailored suit, holding a baby, with a fan blowing my hair back in slow motion. I think I was manifesting being Mariah Carey. TBC. For the next part of the exercise, the smaller picture in the top left-hand corner grows larger and larger, until it fills the whole screen. The starting image now replaces it as a small square in the top left-hand corner. The goal is not to completely remove this starting picture, for its presence resembles awareness and progress. Every night before I went to bed, I would close my eyes, see the large, unattractive image, see the smaller, aspirational one, and then swap them. While I didn't have a label for it at the time, this was undoubtedly my own early experience of visualisation.

The second thing to note is that I knew what I wanted as an outcome, but I had trouble with understanding the journey to the end goal. I could acknowledge that I wanted my life to resemble the more attractive picture. What I didn't have was a fundamental belief that it was possible, or a set of smart systems and processes to help me get there. I'll talk about this more when we discuss goal-setting (see page 225), but for now I'll just say that it's important to have a plan to reach the goal, rather than just to imagine having reached it.

The only way to truly visualise a goal that creates a powerful enough pull is to see, hear, touch, taste and feel that reality. It wasn't enough for me to just see the suit I wanted to wear; I also needed to imagine the colour, the fabric, the cut, the smell. This is where much of the criticism of the idea of manifesting gets it wrong. People who see manifesting as simply imagining a life you want, then sitting back, crossing your fingers and throwing a penny over your shoulder, hoping it happens, miss the point about this meaningful practice. As explained by Roxie Nafousi in her book *Manifest*, the reader has to imagine how they will feel once they've achieved their goal, and to apply as much detail to it as possible. This is a starting point, but it's certainly not all the work. The smartest route to achieving your goals is to create systems and processes that will meaningfully navigate you there. Knowledge of the desired outcome is important, but it is nothing without smart structures.

One of the most meaningful books I have read is *Atomic Habits* by James Clear. In it, he talks about the power of finding alignment with your goal self. In a study of 100 smokers who were attempting to give up smoking, all were offered a cigarette. Those who rejected the cigarette mostly did so with a version of: 'I don't smoke,' while most of those who accepted the cigarette said something like, 'I am trying to give up smoking.' The group who remained steadfast in their commitment to quit identified themselves as non-smokers; they didn't smoke, so why would they have a cigarette? The other group identified themselves as smokers who were attempting to give up, which made them more likely to accept a cigarette.

You can apply the same logic to other things, such as making healthy choices. How would a healthy person behave? They would take the stairs, they would have a rest day, they wouldn't put sugar in their tea. So if you choose to identify as a healthy person, you'll behave like that too. And crucially, in the context of this book, you can ask yourself: how would a successful person behave?

How to *Practise* Visualisation

First, you need to understand what your goal is. For example:

- making £50,000
- being accepted on to a business course
- designing your own work wardrobe
- selling your company
- hiring a certain number of people
- reaching a certain number of followers
- giving up smoking
- moving into your own apartment

Once you are clear with regards to what the goal is, you can hyper-focus on the detail. Think about what achieving that goal would look like, smell like, feel like. Would there be music playing? What is the temperature? Where are you standing, sitting, walking? All these details help bring the picture to life. There's a reason that a synonym for 'visualisation' is 'hallucination'. You are daring to dream of a reality that is deliberately outside your comfort zone, and your brain will naturally revert to your known, lived identity. If, for you, this lived identity is that of someone who feels like a failure, you will continue to create scenarios in which you fail, in order to prove yourself correct. There is a wealth of really interesting reading you can explore on this topic, and it's worth looking up 'self-sabotage' and 'self-fulfilling prophecies' if you'd like to discover more.

One of the best pieces of advice that I have ever been given came from the hugely successful Jo Carr, co-founder of Hope & Glory, who advised me that whenever I make a system or a process, I should think clearly about the behaviour I want to create. How do I want the team to feel, react, behave and respond? Understanding what that looks like helps to sharpen your focus on the best way to do it. Considering the outcome and having a clear picture of how you want it to look, then working backwards to find the best way to achieve it, will help shape the results.

HOW YOU SPEAK TO YOURSELF MATTERS

I'm going to level with you: much of the literature around mental health does not speak to me. As someone who has experienced a wide range of light and shade, I have eagerly listened, talked, read, learned, watched and considered much advice about self-esteem, self-worth, the stories that we write for ourselves and the messages we send. I have actually found it increasingly reductive and unrepresentative to read articles that tell me self-care is taking a bath (spoiler alert, it's not), that taking a duvet day is a basic human right, and that bi-weekly forty-eight-hour tech bans are essential for your wellbeing. The reason for my outright rejection of these extremes is that they are completely impractical for anyone who is a high achiever. Every single person I have ever met who is successful – and there are lots of them – is on a constant journey in pursuit of better, smarter ways to do it all. They accept that resilience is a crucial trait for their success, and they believe strongly in a picture filled with more, not less. I believe that the narrative about how we should look after ourselves is incompatible with the peaks and troughs of our lives.

That said, I did spend twelve-plus years talking to myself like I was a piece of shit on my shoe. Although I had days when I felt that I was maybe one good haircut away from being scouted by a modelling agency, there were also others when I felt that I should live in a way that resembled Stig of the Dump. This oscillation is not uncommon for someone who is burned out and desperate to achieve, but it's fundamentally flawed in the long term.

While I have chosen to not focus on mental health specifically, I feel very strongly – and research would agree – that the way we talk to ourselves matters. A huge shift for me came when I decided to talk to myself like my best friend would. I'd wink at myself in the mirror, I'd pour myself a drink and watch *Girls* when I'd had a bad day at work, and I became my own hype woman. If we are what we repeatedly do, then positivity and kindness are habits that are worth cultivating.

In Brené Brown's best-selling book *Atlas of the Heart*, she writes that confidence is a sense of certainty in our own abilities. Brown wants us to work towards a particular form of confidence that she calls grounded confidence: a powerful sense of self that comes from accurate analysis of what we've done and what we can do. She once walked on stage and playfully warned the crowd that she was genuinely scared for them because of how confident she was.

There is one specific and impactful story that I'd like to share. When I was much younger, I was told a Cherokee legend about two wolves. Stick with me, I promise it's relevant – if it wasn't, it would have been edited out, so don't worry. The story goes like this:

One evening an old Cherokee told his grandson about a battle that goes on inside people.

He said, 'My son, the battle is between two "wolves" inside us all. One is evil. It is anger, envy, jealousy, sorrow, regret, greed, arrogance, self-pity, guilt, resentment, inferiority, lies, false pride, superiority, and ego. The other is good. It is joy, peace, love, hope, serenity, humility, kindness, benevolence, empathy, generosity, truth, compassion and faith.'

The grandson thought about it for a minute and then asked his grandfather: 'Which wolf wins?'

The old Cherokee simply replied, 'The one you feed.'

ABUNDANCE

Abundance is defined as 'a very large quantity of something', and I could confidently say that my twenties provided an abundance of anxiety, self-doubt, limiting beliefs, fear and shame. Quite the cocktail. While we all have a patchwork of personal experiences sewn together to create the tapestry of our lives, many of these feelings are part of systemic, societal and cultural infrastructures that have led us to believe that we have a particular place in the world. There is a reason women find it uncomfortable to talk about money. There is a reason why women hesitate to ask for more, whether at work, in relationships or at home. There is a reason why women take on unpaid work, are often primary caregivers, and seek to reduce feather-ruffling or crowd-dividing. We have been excluded from these conversations – or, to quote *Hamilton*, we've been kept out of 'the room where it happens'. As such, we've been made to accept the idea of being smaller, quieter and less significant, and it has become part of the way in which we represent ourselves. While assessing risk and calculating smart decisions about what you can and can't do is part of succeeding, the fact remains that growing only until we reach the perceived limits of our abilities, indulging in negative thoughts and living in fear will ultimately limit our success.

I shan't tell you to open your heart to the world, to take a bath when it all gets too much, or to stare at yourself in the mirror and repeat, 'I am worthy.' This, to me, feels like advice written by people who have never actually stared down the barrel of extreme self-loathing and thoughts of failure. What I will tell you is that changing your perception to accept the idea that there *is* space for you, space that you never even imagined, and that there *are* opportunities for you and those you care about to succeed, is a huge part of embracing possibility in your professional life. Being honest with yourself about the mindset that you currently have, and then challenging yourself to shift to an abundant mindset, can transform your life. Understanding that there is room for you, and for everyone else, is a key that unlocks enormous potential in becoming more productive and less stressed.

How to *Create* Abundance

Shifting to a mindset of abundance takes discipline. It is a conscious act, and one that you must be committed to. However, no one ever made it big with a scarcity mindset. I can wholeheartedly tell you, there is room for all of us.

A scarcity mindset is characterised by a belief that one has limited resources or is unable to provide for themselves or others.

How do you know if you have a scarcity mindset? Are these good descriptions of your behaviour?

- thinking you always lose and others always win
- viewing others as competitors
- being overly controlling
- being pessimistic
- feeling like you're always behind
- being impatient
- overscheduling yourself
- feeling depressed or paralysed
- saying yes to opportunities that aren't right for you because you fear you won't receive other opportunities
- struggling with concentration
- feeling dissatisfied
- experiencing low self-esteem
- believing you're not enough
- comparing yourself to others

An abundant mindset, on the other hand, is one in which you believe there is enough for everyone. The success of others does not make you feel jealous or fearful. Their success does not detract from your own, and you genuinely want to see others achieve their goals.

Here's how to switch from a scarcity mindset to an abundant mindset:

- Foster collaborative relationships. Your environment matters.
- Practise gratitude. Gratitude can help you be aware of what you do have, instead of fixating on what you don't.
- Notice and redirect negative automatic thoughts.
- Practise self-compassion.
- Speak to yourself like your best friend would.
- Become overprotective of your own time.
- Remember that everything you do and think takes energy. Use it on the things that matter.
- Find a mindfulness practice that works for you.
- Drop the guilt.
- Compare yourself to yourself.

'The mind is everything. What you think, you become.'

How to *Invite In* Abundant Thoughts

Let's imagine you are looking to move jobs. With a scarcity mindset, you might experience thoughts such as:

- The market is really tough right now.

- I won't be paid what I want.
- Am I good enough to work at the company I want to?
- There will probably be lots of more qualified candidates.
- What if I go for it and don't get hired?

By switching to an abundance mindset, your thoughts might be more like this:

- This is the package I deserve: salary, flexibility, title.
- I have the experience to add a huge amount of value to this new role.
- In tough markets, strong candidates are even more valuable.
- If I don't get the job, the rejection is just redirection.
- I'll no doubt learn a huge amount from the process.

Be Your *Own* Hype Woman

If you are experiencing a situation that is making you anxious, stressed, down, sad or frustrated, identify three things that your best friend would need in this situation:

1. ______________________________
2. ______________________________
3. ______________________________

Now write down why you haven't offered those things to yourself:

1. ______________________________
2. ______________________________
3. ______________________________

WHO YOU SURROUND YOURSELF WITH MATTERS

I have done the legwork, trying all sorts of mainstream and more whack-a-doodle methods to try and move myself forward on my journey. My forays into the weird and wonderful have usually been related to the state of my mental health at that time. A personal low point was entertaining the idea that there was a poltergeist living inside me that was trapped there due to a series of unresolved business deals in a previous life. Paying a woman cash in her house in Harrow on a Saturday morning while she spoke to the business spirits seemed, at the time, like a really, really good idea.

While this was a bit extreme, something I do strongly believe in is that energy attracts energy – that what comes directly to you is a result of what you put out into the world. In very basic terms, the people I have met at my lowest times vibrated at a lower frequency than those I met when entertaining abundance. If you are only open to average opportunities, your brain will automatically reject situations in which you might be exposed to anything other than that. In her enormously successful book *Daring Greatly*, Brené Brown tells us not to move through the world looking for examples as to why you shouldn't exist – because you'll always find them.

Critical to success is the practice of opening yourself to possibilities. Doing this starts with making four key changes:

1. Audit who you spend your time with.
2. Ferociously protect your own peace.
3. Be accountable.
4. Practise gratitude.

Tony Robbins once said: 'The quality of a person's life is most often a direct reflection of the expectations of their peer group.' It's important to ensure that the people you spend time with, those you let into your life, are reflective of the person you want to be.

WISE WORDS, SMART SWAPS

The language you choose to use is important. Every time you consider an action, you are sending yourself a message. Given that the messages we send ourselves matter in shaping outcomes, it's integral to the Smarter Method to review the language you are choosing to use and what you are communicating through the words you choose to use. Holding yourself accountable for the way in which you are viewing a situation, and how that shapes the outcome, is an important part of switching to an abundant mindset. Here are some smart swaps to consider making.

Instead of saying ...	Try saying ...
'I have to go to the gym.'	'I get to go to the gym.'
'I have to stay late at work.'	'I'm putting in the work.'
'I didn't get the job.'	'I'm being redirected to the next opportunity.'
'They said no.'	'I had the courage to ask.'

GUT INSTINCT

The main thing to remember about your gut is this: that bitch is your friend. She wants the best for you, she's looking out for you, and although she might have warned you a million times, she will still be there when you inevitably fuck it up and go against her; she'll still be rooting for you just as aggressively as the first time.

In order to prove that these aren't just the ramblings of a mad woman, there is some science that supports the gut–brain connection.

Research tells us that what we experience as intuition is in fact our brain recalling past experiences at super speed and combining these with environmental cues in the present to help us make a decision. Essentially, all that we've experienced before is analysed, set against the real-time environment, and a decision is made. This happens outside of our conscious awareness, which is why it can be challenging to trust. There is a deep neurological basis for intuition and it's the reason scientists refer to our gut as the 'second brain'. As such, our brain is constantly making assessments in conversation with the gut in order to inform the situation we find ourselves in.

The issue in my experience isn't that the gut doesn't talk to us. Mine's a chatty Cathy. I have fantastic intuition, and many of the successful people I have met have had a high EQ (emotional intelligence) and refer often to their 'gut feelings'. The issue is not the gut failing to give us an answer, it's that we sometimes make the decision to go against that answer.

The Smarter Method encourages you to embrace the idea that things don't have to be as hard as we have been led to believe they do. Most of us have all the tools we need at our fingertips, and making small tweaks can create a seismic shift. Good decision-making is inherently about making the goddamn decision. Providing momentum. When we become aware of our instinctive decision, there is often a space between acknowledging this and acting on it, and this manifests as procrastination. While it is important to consider alternative viewpoints, gather facts and make informed decisions, once you have all of this, your gut will speak to you. Overthinking, not trusting your gut, and ultimately delaying decisions comes from a lack of faith in your gut feeling, and a nervousness that leaves you unwilling to make the decision.

With that in mind, here are five key steps to embracing your gut instinct.

How to Embrace Your *Gut Instinct*

1. **Write down your initial reaction.** This has been hugely beneficial for my enhanced gut-trusting practice. If I am delaying making a decision, or allowing too many additional opinions to distract me, I can end up confusing myself into decision paralysis. If I immediately write down what I think, I always have the reference point of what my gut wanted me to do.
2. **Filter other opinions.** Being given advice or information to help us make a decision can be helpful, providing us with a sense check or an alternative point of view. But it can also be unhelpful. Too many competing opinions can make you doubt yourself, delay your decision-making and overthink things. It's important to keep the circle tight and not invite too many people into that process.
3. **Connect with yourself.** I get it, what the fuck does that even mean? Isn't the whole point that if you're not trusting your gut, then you aren't connected? Well, yes. Meditation and mindfulness, or whatever other marketing language you'd prefer, are key when it comes

to connecting with your gut. I prefer the term 'stillness'. Stillness provides a quiet space in which I can truly consider what I think and feel. Stillness helps train your awareness and build a healthy sense of perspective.

4. **Feel the feels.** Our emotions and feelings might not only be an important part of our intuitive ability to make good decisions; they may actually be essential.
5. **Remember that your gut is looking out for you.** Henry Mintzberg, professor of management at McGill University and a longtime proponent of intuitive decision-making, says the sense of revelation at the obvious occurs when your conscious mind finally learns something that your subconscious mind had already known.[1]

Signs of a *Gut Feeling*

- a flash of clarity
- tension or tightness in your body
- goosebumps or prickling
- 'butterflies' or nausea
- a sinking sensation in the pit of your stomach
- sweaty palms or feet

- thoughts that keep returning to a specific person or situation
- feelings of peace, safety or happiness (after making a decision)

YOU DON'T NEED TO BE 100 PER CENT SURE

In the ten seconds that wasn't ranting masculine energy, I heard something about this on a Joe Rogan podcast. It really resonated with me, and has helped me immeasurably in terms of becoming a better decision-maker. I've spent most of my life being encouraged to provide 100 per cent accuracy and commitment to big decisions: 'Are you absolutely sure?', 'Are you 100 per cent sure?'

The pressure that this puts on decision-making actually misguides the decision-maker and leaves them focusing on the wrong part of the decision. With the long lists of decisions that need to be made by those in business, indecision is the most paralysing state to be in. Purgatory, if you will. The ability to create momentum, and thus the ability to move forward, is a key skill. Whether ultimately the decision made turns out to be a perfect one or a good one is largely irrelevant. It's the ability to make the decision that is the skill.

With many of the decisions that have been difficult for me to make, I can attribute that difficulty to a desire to be 100 per cent sure. But I have realised over the course of my career, and particularly since the Covid-19 pandemic, that the goal isn't actually to be finite, complete and 100 per cent sure about the decision. Rather, I just needed to be sure *enough*.

Of course, one must factor in a series of considerations and not become reckless, but here are some examples of where being 100 per cent sure doesn't matter.

- I'm not 100 per cent sure that I rented the best office I could for my business. But I am more than 80 per cent sure.
- I'm not 100 per cent sure that the promotion I recently gave will succeed in every way I imagined, but I'm more than 50 per cent sure.
- I am not 100 per cent sure that the new branding for my business is the best branding I could have chosen, but I'm more than 50 per cent sure.
- I am not 100 per cent sure that I chose the perfect name for my agency. But it's good enough.

This method is not about the acceptance of mediocrity. It is not about doing 'just enough'. Rather, it is about understanding that in order to create momentum and movement in your business, you have to move through decisions in a way that feels decisive. You have to consider the message you send with the decisions you make. If you make the wrong decision, there will be another one to make shortly after, and if you make the right decision, there will be another one too. The goal is not to make the perfect decision every time, nor to be 100 per cent sure that it's the right decision. The goal is to be sure enough, and to be able to move forward.

THINGS TO REMEMBER ON YOUR JOURNEY TO SUCCESS

No One *Cares* As Much As You

Running a business or committing passionately to your job can consume an enormous amount of energy and time.

I believe that successful people have two competing qualities. The first is an immeasurable sense of self-doubt and fear of failure. The second is an overwhelming sense that they have something of huge value to offer the world. It is at the intersection of these two qualities that great things can be accomplished. This is an important point. In order to achieve great things, you must have a passion and drive that enables you to invest in yourself: a drive to show up. It is not about eliminating that feeling; rather, it is about managing it and making it work for you. It is about harnessing these feelings in a smarter way.

I started my business at twenty-two years old. I did have businesses before that, but all were helping me learn how to run my current agency. I spent the entirety of my twenties consumed by my job. It trumped everything: family weddings, dates, Christmas Day, my own health. It was all I did, all I thought about and all I talked about. I felt that I had no value outside of my work, nothing to contribute beyond a dialogue about my job, and no interest in or energy for anything else. I gave absolutely everything I had to my career, and I wanted to talk to people about it. It was the most important thing in my world. Decisions felt like make or break, and tough times felt like live or die. I struggled with the fact that no one else seemed to understand me. It was my dad who forced me to gain some perspective on this. He told me: 'No one cares as much as you do.' He suggested that it was right that I was more tired than others, that I should eat last in the team, and that my finances were more precarious. He reminded me that I had chosen this, but that it was no more important to anyone else than their own job.

It is important to manage your expectations of others as you continue on your journey of achieving your career goals. No doubt there will be sacrifices along the way that will feel huge to you, but retaining a sense of perspective allows you to remember that you are on your own journey, and it's not as important to everyone else around you.

Variety *Is* Key

When all your focus is on your work, it can be overwhelming. Although hard work is important, it's crucial to have other things in your life in order to avoid burnout. Having variety in the things to which you apply your brain ensures that you aren't totally consumed by work, and it will probably enhance your relationships. When focusing on being smarter in this sense, ask yourself the following questions.

- How many of my spare hours are consumed with thinking about, talking about or doing work?

- When was the last time I felt relaxed and present, and what was I doing at the time?
- Am I changing my environment enough? For example, am I getting out into nature if I live in a city?
- What is preventing me from being present in moments that should be enjoyable?
- Why is work always on my mind?
- Who am I spending most of my time with?
- Am I consuming a variety of music, podcasts and literature?
- Am I doing something daily for myself that isn't work-related?

The mark of success is not to be more tired than everyone else, nor is it to be so committed to your work that you can't engage with or enjoy anything else. It is not about being busier than everyone else or focusing all your time on your job.

There are a number of ways in which you can carve out time for yourself and your brain. Engaging with a variety of different things is ultimately what will keep you more balanced. Here are some ideas.

- Expose yourself to a variety of films, television shows, books, audiobooks, podcasts and content that has nothing to do with your job, on topics such as history, comedy or cooking.
- Create better boundaries with regards to how and where you talk about your job, and be accountable for

what you talk about outside of the office.

- Read the room; your friends who don't run companies are probably less interested in hearing about your weekly work woes.
- Open your mind to the idea that variety will ultimately help you remain more balanced.
- Find time to be present and grateful for the current experience you are having, rather than thinking about the next twenty-four hours.
- View variety as abundance, not as a burden.

CHAPTER 3

Minutes

'Until you value yourself, you will not value your time.'

M. SCOTT PECK

Competitive time-management has become a focus of much conversation online and in the workplace. The approach I have seen most frequently tends to involve setting an alarm earlier and earlier in order to create additional hours in the day, rather than more carefully spending the ones that are already available. You may have been told that you need to develop better time-management skills, or to make your time work harder for you, but without being given any guidance on how to do that. In this chapter, we'll explore practical ways to master your time, including running your day in minutes, discovering the added benefits of desk timers, learning how to time-block, and understanding why boundary-setting is key to unlocking productivity. This chapter will help arm you with realistic and usable daily systems for managing your minutes.

WHAT IS TIME-MANAGEMENT?

Managing time has become an overcomplicated, almost abstract concept, but it doesn't have to be. Time-management simply means:

- predicting how long something will take
- sticking to the predicted times
- fitting the tasks into the time that you have
- matching the energy you have to the tasks you need to complete

Time-management, simply put, is an organisational challenge. If tackled correctly, it can help you feel like you are more in control of your time, and more productive as a consequence. Many of the skills you are learning in this book come back to great time-management.

To understand what it is that you have to do in order to master this relatively boring topic, you must first understand where you currently are. Start by answering these questions:

- How good am I at organising my time?
- How often do I miss deadlines?
- How often do I end up running late despite planning ahead?

- Am I setting myself deadlines, or are they being set for me (by a manager, for example)?
- How do I feel when I miss a deadline?
- How often do I feel as though I have completed all my work?

For many of us, our focus has been on squeezing as much as we can into tight time frames. Everything feels urgent, and it's a race to get things done as quickly as possible. It's a grown-up version of 'I'll pull an all-nighter to finish this dissertation if I have to.' The long-term problem with this approach is that it's a one-way ticket to burnout. Although every so often, it's appropriate to pull out all the stops to get something done, it should definitely be an exception, not a rule. The Smarter Method asks you to reframe your approach. Instead of thinking about fitting in as much as possible, it's time to think about realistic time frames for the work you have to complete. Good time-management requires a shift in focus from *activities* to *results*. Being busy isn't the same as being effective. In fact, for many people, the busier they are, the less they actually achieve.

A common mistake is that we don't actually consider how long things will take. Because we are stressed and frazzled and have a perception of time scarcity, the outcome is always a race to see how much we can complete in the time we have.

Rather than focusing on the time you have, and importing an entire to-do list into that time frame, making it work at all costs, try starting with the task instead. How long will the task actually take? With some of the most successful people I have worked with, I've seen that they have an ability to realistically predict how long tasks will take, and then allocate the correct amount of time to the task. They focus on the desired results for the job at hand. In order to get better at predicting how long tasks will take, you could try time-tracking.

TRACKING YOUR TIME

Timesheet tools are a great way to create accountability for your time. Time-tracking is a simple way of reviewing where your time has gone, and inspiring you to make changes should that pattern not be desirable. You should see this as a review of your time. Commit to tracking your time for a month, in the same way you would write down what you eat in a diet diary. I'd suggest updating your timesheet daily, otherwise you tend to fill it in aspirationally, which means you're lying to yourself. Once you've tracked your time for a month, you will have a realistic view of where your time and energy goes. You'll be horrified that some tasks took so long; others you'll feel you could probably do slightly faster, and a few you may realise could have been delegated. Looking ahead to the next month (or week, if that is more manageable), try to apply this new knowledge and allocate desirable times to the tasks you need to complete. Knowing where you are before you start creating a plan of where you want to get to is an important part of working smarter. This will also help you begin to track your energy better. Allocating time for specific tasks is all part of setting better boundaries, protecting your mindset and setting realistic deadlines.

Here is an example of a to-do list with times attached:

Task	Time required
Write press release	30 minutes
Review new business contract	55 minutes
Review social media plan	45 minutes
Write a LinkedIn post	15 minutes
Write agenda for Monday morning meeting	10 minutes

You can convert your weekly timesheet into a helpful pie chart to see whether you are really spending your time the way you want to.

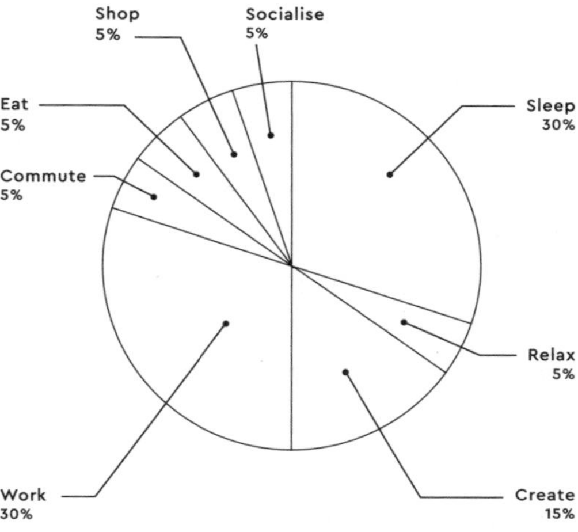

TIMERS

If you make one investment, other than your copy of this book (thank you) and multiple copies for your friends and colleagues (also thank you), it should be in a desk timer. Desk timers look and feel suspiciously close to kitchen timers, but we are where we are.

Desk timers are transformational. They are the single best way to bring awareness to your time-management, and provide transparency as to where your time is going. In addition, they are a crucial part of encouraging you to take needed breaks throughout the day, something which is often forgotten in the desperate race to dusk. Depending on which research journal you review, scientists put our ability to concentrate at anywhere between ten and fifty-two minutes. You can naturally gauge this for yourself, using your timer to identify how regularly you lose focus and start procrastinating. My concentration span sits at about forty minutes on average. As such, I won't ever allocate more than forty minutes at a time, to any given task, even if that means I have to revisit it later on that day, or that week.

While desk timers can help you to determine your concentration window, their best use is to help you stick to the times you have allocated for your tasks throughout the day. Setting yourself a timed task creates a completion loop that helps improve focus and avoid distractions.

Once you have written out your tasks for the day and

allocated a suggested time (ideally no longer than your own concentration limit), you can begin your first task. Set the timer to the specific number of minutes you have allocated to this task, then get started. Most people are surprised by how quickly the timer goes off. This is a good thing. It's bringing awareness to the shape of your day, and helping you to improve your time-management. If you haven't finished your task by the time the timer goes off, try and predict how much longer it will take you. If you think you need an extra twenty minutes, set the timer for twenty minutes. If you successfully complete the task using that additional time, you'll know for next time how to set a more realistic time frame for that particular task.

Tips on *Timers*

- Use a desk timer, not your phone.
- Close all tabs, apps or open docs that do not relate to the task at hand.
- Test and learn; you might need to adjust the set timings in the first week of trying this new tool. Adaptability is important.
- See if you can find a timer with a pleasant alarm at the end of the set time. I personally do not find it encouraging to hear a sound like a nuclear siren to mark the end of my allocated time period.
- Bring awareness to the practice. Set boundaries with others so they know not to interrupt you during these timed tasks, so that you can set yourself up to win.

The *Pomodoro* Technique

This technique was developed by Francesco Cirillo in the late 1980s, when he was a student. Struggling to focus on his studies and finding it difficult to complete his work on time, Francesco needed a solution. He decided to commit to two-minute intervals of pure focused study. In an attempt to increase his success rate and create some accountability, he found a kitchen timer in the shape of a tomato (pomodoro in Italian). Each time he succeeded, he would reset the timer and challenge himself to a longer period of uninterrupted study. Through trial and error, he found that the most effective approach was twenty-fiveminutes of focus followed by a five-minute break. This method is still widely used today.

TIME-BLOCKING

Time-blocking is a well-covered topic in the world of productivity. It asks that you divide your day into blocks of time. Each block is dedicated to accomplishing a specific task or group of tasks, and only those specific tasks. Time-blocking requires you to have a strong sense of the tasks at hand that day, an ability to predict how long they will take, and a commitment to fitting them into the time you have allocated. The reason time-blocking is popular is because it helps you to protect your time and your focus simultaneously.

What Does *Time-Blocking* Look Like?

Very simply put, time-blocking involves the following steps:

- Identifying the list of tasks for the day.
- Labelling them in terms of prioritisation.
- Matching the tasks to your energy, allocating the more challenging tasks to the times at which you usually have more energy.
- Allocating a number of minutes to each task.
- Setting up your timer to reflect the minutes you have allocated to the first task, and begin.

Instead of keeping an open-ended to-do list of things you'll get to 'as soon as you can', you'll start each day with a concrete schedule outlining what you'll work on and when. For smaller tasks, you can use the ten-second test (see page 48) to batch tasks together, and tick them off your list quickly and efficiently.

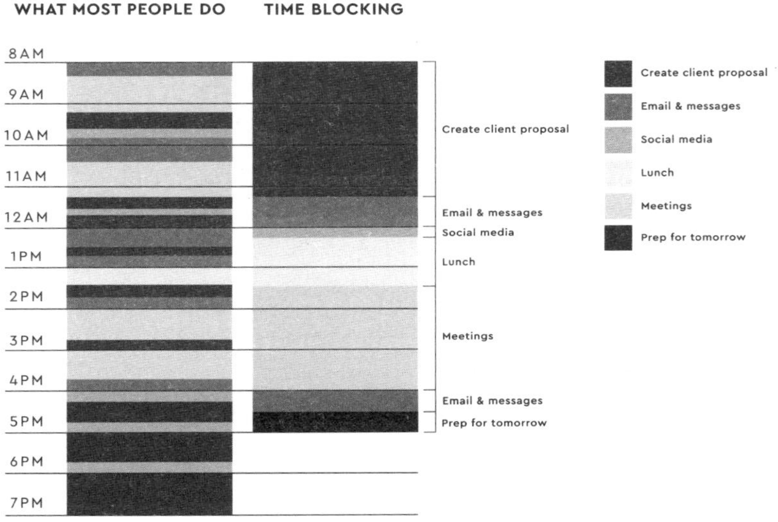

Time-blocking can help provide strong boundaries for your team, and shift the mindset from volume to impact. For example, if you find yourself endlessly reviewing documents, reading copy and approving images, at all hours of the day, you may decide to have a one-hour 'review time' between 11am and 12pm, during which you dedicate your time to reviewing, giving feedback and signing off documents. If your team is able to have the relevant documents with you before that time, they will be reviewed that day. If not, they will roll into tomorrow's review time. We will discuss boundaries further on page 92, but it is important to ensure that your time works for you.

What Are the *Benefits* of Time-Blocking?

Time-blocking:

- gives you a greater sense of autonomy and control over your time
- helps with setting boundaries
- promotes a flow state (more about this in Chapter 9)
- encourages mono-tasking, which in turn improves focus
- leads to better diary management

Remember: being busy is not the same as being productive.

THE 480-MINUTE DAY

This is a form of time-blocking where, instead of thinking about how many hours you have in a working day, you look at how many *minutes* you have:

Number of hours in the working day x 60 minutes = number of minutes

So, if you're working an average eight-hour day, you have 480 minutes to complete your work tasks. This is only a third of the time available to you in a twenty-four-hour period. (If you are reading this thinking that your working hours usually take up much more of your thoughts than the other sixteen hours, you might be a good candidate for a Busyness Detox (see page 202).)

I switched from the eight-hour day to the 480-minute day in an effort to plan my days better and allocate time to specific work tasks. I was coming up against repeated frustrations such as missing deadlines, poor planning and always feeling as though I could go home and continue work. Granted, as a business owner, there are many times when working on a weekend or in the evening is an essential part of achieving success. However, whether you're an ambitious go-getter, a young mother or a dynamic dreamer, this is not an effective long-term plan.

To begin, sit in the morning with a piece of paper or a blank document, and write down your list of tasks for the day. The next step is to identify which of the tasks are urgent and important, remembering that you should focus on a maximum of three important tasks per day. Those tasks you deem less important can be reallocated using what you will learn in the 'Eliminate or Delegate' section (see page 150). Once you have your considered to-do list, allocate minutes for each task, making sure your total is no more than 480 minutes.

Benefits of the *480-Minute* Day

- You can work more effectively by being realistic with the time you have for the tasks at hand.
- You are more likely to stick to deadlines.
- You are less likely to waste time. If you are working in hour-long time blocks, you might allocate a one-hour window to complete a task that will only take

you forty minutes, and it's then common to waste the remaining twenty minutes of that hour. When you are planning in minutes, you don't allocate excess time.

- Everyone has a different limit to their concentration, be aware of yours.
- It breeds accountability. Being a good manager is about being reliable. Poor management skills encourage you to take ownership of everything, which can ultimately lead to a poorer quality of work and chaotic working patterns. Through allocating your minutes per day, you gain a much better grasp on the available time you have, and you are therefore less likely to overcommit.
- It creates a stronger sense of what your team can expect from you.
- You will feel an increased sense of calm in the face of your workload.
- You will have a greater ability to say no if you do not have the time to complete a task, because you will know right away whether you have the time available.
- You will be more productive.

BOUNDARIES

Throughout my fifteen-year career, my relationship with boundaries has evolved. Simply put, I once had none, and now I not only have them, but I protect them with the global power of a thousand-ship fleet. My goal is for you to discover, set and enforce boundaries in a way that will truly transform your work and personal life. Boundaries can be a way to protect yourself and your time. Looking back I wasted time travelling to places I didn't want to go, taking on work I didn't want to do, attending parties I didn't want to be at, and enduring relationships I didn't want to be in. Protecting and feeling in control of your time, and thus spending it on people, places and things that truly make you more fulfilled, is an invaluable life skill.

Early on in my career, I found myself scratching my head as I repeatedly came up against these experiences:

- I felt as worthless as a piece of shit on your shoe, and would therefore attempt to continually shine as brightly as a supernova until my bosses noticed me, while simultaneously disregarding metaphors about literally burning out.
- I thought I could bypass 'the work', and be an anomaly in creating a successful life.
- I was routinely underpaid for the work I did, with budgets that I had set myself.
- I was routinely inconvenienced by social, travel, personal and professional plans.
- No ask was too great. I would have agreed to be a client's surrogate had they asked on the weekly call.
- I assumed that I wasn't the obvious choice, always, and felt shame in connection with this.

For my first ever internship, I worked for a London-based PR company (which I shan't name, but if you message me directly, I will almost certainly spill the tea). In between licking stamps, rebinding printed press coverage, unpacking samples and wondering what my future would hold, I was asked to go and see the boss, a formidable middle-aged woman with a penchant for a fake bag and a shrill, metallic tone. I'll set the scene. It was 5pm, thirty-five degrees, and I was wearing a pair of fur-lined boots that had been gifted to me by the agency in lieu of payment (omg, thank you SO MUCH!). They were a size too small. I wore them to prove I was grateful and that my toes needed accountability.

The boss gave me this exciting brief: 'I have eight people coming for dinner at my house this evening. I'd like you to go to the house, turn on the oven, head to the shop and buy ingredients, return to the house, lay them out, then set the table, so that when I get home, it's all ready for me to go.'

She gave me £10 for the ingredients. Now, I'm not old enough for this to be one of those situations where Baby Boomers bought a house for a tenner and a packet of Polos, only for that house to now be worth over a million (and then they ask us why none of us are yet on the property ladder). The £10 she gave me is pretty much the same as £10 now. Of course, I completed the task, and am ashamed to admit that I paid, with my own money, the difference between her pathetic contribution and the actual cost of the ingredients for a dinner for eight people. It goes without saying that I didn't even know what a boundary was back then, let alone have the tool kit to set and enforce healthy boundaries.

Boundaries can be tricky to navigate. Should you be required to go into work at 8am if you're only being paid from 9am? These sorts of questions have flooded social media in recent years, and rightly so.

The important point here is that it's all about context. For a business that gives you brilliant benefits, a fantastic workplace, flexibility and a supportive team, you may feel inclined to show up a bit earlier, and agree to the occasional request to demonstrate your commitment to the business and your gratitude for what they have provided you with. For a business that does the opposite, naturally you will feel less inclined to invest your time and energy beyond what you are contracted to do. These issues can be divisive, because they are deeply personal. My boundaries are different to yours. My tolerance is different to yours. My challenges are different to yours. And these differences are found in multiple variations across multiple people. We must, if nothing else, try to respect and understand one another's reasons for the boundaries we each set.

This, however, assumes that you are in control of your boundaries – which, spoiler alert, you probably aren't. So, let's go back a step.

Why Are *Boundaries* Important?

People treat you as you allow them to treat you. The mastery of healthy boundaries is one of the most valuable techniques demonstrated by successful people. Entire books have been, and no doubt will continue to be, written about them. Intrinsically, boundaries are incredibly personal, and are tethered unwaveringly to our own sense of self-esteem, and self-confidence.

So, What Is a *Healthy* Boundary?

Much of the self-help literature available encourages us to unlearn systems and processes that we have been taught from a young age. The Smarter Method asks you to work *with* them. Many of us have been encouraged to show empathy for others: to consider other people's feelings, religions, preferences, ideologies and patterns. Many of us have developed significant social skills to be able to show up for others – often, before we'll show up for ourselves. Although compassionate living is an important skill, there is a danger that as we get older, the success of others can also correspond to our own discomfort. Many of us aren't comfortable setting or enforcing boundaries because we struggle with the concept of showing up for ourselves. We fear the outcome of the boundary not being respected, or the rejection that might come from being upfront about our boundary.

Here are some examples of the anxieties we might feel around boundaries.

- 'If I ask for the pay I believe is appropriate for this job, it might be more than the other candidate asks for, so I might not get the role.'
- 'If I don't agree to travel across town for the date, the person I am going on a date with might cancel.'

- 'If I don't pay for dinner, my friends won't want to hang out with me.'
- 'If I don't finish my colleague's work for them, it might affect my promotion or they will think I'm not a team player.'

Our understanding of selfishness tends to dictate that acts that serve us are inherently bad. However, an individual understanding, accepting and setting boundaries does not stand to harm another individual in any way. It's not about forcing anyone else to change their behaviour, and success is not based on the other individual respecting your boundaries. Success here is your own ability to connect with the identified boundaries that enhance your own work–life balance, and you having the confidence to enforce them. The challenge is that we exist within a matrix that suggests that we either deserve or don't deserve boundaries. The worse our self-esteem is, the less deserving we are of success and respect.

Healthy boundaries are the limits you place around your time, emotions, body and mental health in order to stay resilient and happy. They protect you from being used, drained or manipulated by others. A person with healthy boundaries understands that making their expectations clear helps in two ways: it establishes what behaviour they will accept from other people, and it establishes what behaviour other people can expect from them. Boundaries offer clarity for everyone involved.

Imagine that I am buying a house next door to you. If at no point does anyone draw specifically for me the land boundary, how do I know where my land ends and yours begins? How do I know where there is gate access, whether there is a public footpath, which parking space I am entitled to? Once you can draw your own boundaries, you can begin to consider access. Some people may have none. Some may have a gate code, some a key. Until you know precisely what these boundaries are, it is impossible to uphold them.

Generally speaking, there are five types of boundary:

1. **Physical.** These boundaries relate to your personal space, your privacy and your body.
2. **Sexual.** These relate to your expectations concerning intimacy.
3. **Intellectual.** These boundaries concern your thoughts and beliefs. Intellectual boundaries are not respected when someone dismisses another person's ideas and opinions.
4. **Emotional.** These relate to a person's feelings.
5. **Financial.** These boundaries might relate to your salary, lending money to others or what you're willing to spend your money on.

Most of us have a mixture of different types of boundaries, and they are often dependent on context and our own self-confidence within the specific area. If someone has low self-esteem, this can correlate to looser sexual boundaries. If someone has strong financial competence, they might have rigid boundaries in this space.

How Do I *Identify* My Boundaries?

- Connect with your gut. Even if you aren't able to fully identify or uphold your boundaries, your body has the ability to tell you when something isn't in alignment.
- If you experience a negative emotion, this can often be a sign of a boundary having been crossed or not honoured.
- Are there areas of your life that you feel you are nailing? If so, what are the reasons for that? These are the things you should be doing more of, and are likely areas that you've already enforced boundaries in.
- If a situation makes you feel unsafe or taken advantage of, that can be a sign that one of your boundaries has been crossed.
- Ask others about their boundaries. Hearing stories of boundaries set by others can provide useful inspiration for identifying your own.
- Connect with your values; they will relate to your boundaries.

Why *Connecting with Your Values* is Necessary for Boundary-Setting

As I'm sure you now know, for much of my twenties I felt totally unanchored and confused about who I was and what was truly important to me. And let me tell you, it's very difficult to identify and enforce boundaries, truly live abundantly, seek opportunities that you feel in total alignment with and learn to trust your gut if you are not tethered to a value system. As I approached my twenty-eighth birthday, I felt totally valueless. I couldn't provide answers to what seemed like the most basic questions: Where did I want to live? What haircut did I want? What fulfilled me at work? Did I want children? Who did I want to date? What was my fashion style? What music did I like? What did I do for fun? I felt as though I was drifting and didn't really know myself at all.

Our values are our own set of internal guiding principles for the way we want to live our lives. They are not set in stone and can evolve over time. What I know now, and what I want to tell you is, if you feel how I did as I approached twenty-eight, it's not because you are valueless. It's because the values that served you for the years that preceded have been outgrown. It's time to discover a set of values that truly reflect how you feel about the world around you and your place in it.

Values are unlike goals or intentions we set for ourselves. They aren't something to achieve or something to be checked off a list, but instead are core beliefs that guide us in every aspect of our life and the decisions that we make in regard to how we spend our time, money and attention. They serve as a foundation for who we want to be and what is most important to us.

This is a deeply personal exercise and requires some thought. It might be something that you come back to, and it might be a task where the answers don't immediately appear.

The first step is to answer the questions below:

1. When was I the happiest in my life?
2. What am I most proud of?
3. What am I currently spending most of my spare time doing?
4. If the things I am currently doing in my spare time are not things I feel super energised by, what would I prefer to be doing instead?
5. What is important to me?
6. How do I want others to describe me?
7. What would make me walk away from a friendship?
8. What would make me walk away from a romantic relationship?
9. What qualities do I admire in others?

Once you have answered these questions, part two is to really refine the words that best represent your answers, in order to better clarify what is important to you.

From the list below, circle or highlight every word that resonates with you. Don't overthink the selection. As you look at the words, identify the ones that feel like they are connected to you, how you are or how you want to be showing up. If a word comes up for you that is not on the below list, you can add it. You can select as many words as you like.

Abundance	Compassion	Gratitude	Learning	Resourcefulness
Acceptance	Consistency	Growth	Lenience	Respect
Accountability	Control	Happiness	Love	Responsibility
Adaptability	Cooperation	Health	Loyalty	Risk
Adventure	Creativity	Honesty	Mindfulness	Safety
Altruism	Curiosity	Humility	Openness	Security
Aspiration	Daring	Humour	Optimism	Simplicity
Assertiveness	Decisiveness	Independence	Originality	Spirituality
Autonomy	Dependability	Individuality	Passion	Stability
Balance	Diversity	Innovation	Peace	Success
Boundaries	Empathy	Inspiration	Perfectionism	Teamwork
Brilliance	Enthusiasm	Integrity	Playfulness	Thoughtfulness
Calm	Fairness	Intelligence	Popularity	Trust
Caution	Flexibility	Intuition	Power	Versatility
Challenge	Freedom	Iridescence	Preparation	Vision
Charity	Friendship	Joy	Professionalism	Warmth
Commitment	Fun	Knowledge	Punctuality	Wealth
Community	Generosity	Leadership	Reflection	Wisdom

Once you have highlighted your chosen words, go through and see if you can categorise them into different families – you want five maximum. Each group will be subjective and based on your own experience so don't worry about making all of them perfectly even.

Next, pick the word in each grouping that feels most representative to you – this will be your hero word. You should end up with something like this:

Abundance	**Acceptance**	Trust	**Balance**	Humour
Gratitude	Compassion	Teamwork	Health	Fun
Freedom	Loyalty	Openness	Wellbeing	Playfulness
Peace	Intuition	Friendship	Spirituality	**Warmth**
Independence	Kindness	Cooperation	Mindfulness	Community
Flexibility	Reflection	**Empathy**	Growth	Adventure
Security	Honesty		Thoughtfulness	Altruism
Calm				
Wisdom				

You can now add a verb to each value to create an actionable core value, so you should end up with something like this:

- Live in abundance.
- Seek opportunities where I can empower others.
- Act with mindfulness.
- Promote teamwork.
- Multiply empathy.

Finally, organise your core values in order of priority (most important to least important). Post your reorganised list somewhere easily visible so that it's available as an easy reference when you are faced with decisions.

Hard *and* Soft Boundaries

When defining boundaries, it may help to separate them into hard and soft boundaries.

Hard boundaries are things you find non-negotiable and will not compromise on. They are those 'make or break' situations: things you will never accept or do. We will return to this a bit later.

Soft boundaries are more flexible; they're things you're willing to compromise on, negotiate about or accept (within reason). You can think of soft boundaries like wishes or setting goals.

If someone crosses a soft boundary, you might be willing to overlook it, engage with the person, communicate with them, or gently remind them of how you'd prefer to work together in the future. Hard boundaries differ in that they are linked to your value system, and have harsher personal consequences for you.

For many of us, identifying boundaries isn't the difficult part. It's usually enforcing or maintaining them that can be tricky. I found it quite easy to connect with what my boundaries were; however, I repeatedly allowed others to trample all over them as a consequence of my scarcity mindset, as I valued myself very little.

How to *Maintain* Your Boundaries

- **Remember your reasons.** Think about the reasons you set the boundary in the first place.

- **Consider the alternative.** I would say with confidence that although it can be difficult to stick to your boundaries in the moment, the alternative is always worse. Revisit the examples on page 96:
    - 'If I ask for the pay I believe is appropriate for this job, it might be more than the other candidate asks for, so I might not get the role.' *If you do get the job, you will be working for less than you feel you deserve, in a role that doesn't see your value or potential.*
    - 'If I don't agree to travel across town for the date, the person I am going on a date with might cancel.' *If you do go, you will be engaging in a relationship with someone on an unbalanced basis, expecting that you need to literally go the distance for them to be interested in you, and assuming that any mild friction might turn them off you.*
    - 'If I don't pay for dinner, my friends won't want to hang out with me.' *If you do pay, you are creating a situation based on you providing monetary value for your friends.*
    - 'If I don't finish my colleague's work for them, it might affect my promotion, or they will think I'm not a team player.' *In the long term, this attitude could mean you are likely to not finish your own work or underperform, which might lead you to miss out on a pay rise or a promotion, and poorly manage and train your juniors.*

- **Start small.** Don't overwhelm yourself. Start with a few smaller boundaries that you feel safe or comfortable enforcing.
- **Ask for help.** Ask your manager at work to provide training for you, include boundary-setting in your yearly objectives, and read and research recommended literature that helps you better understand the topic.
- **Work on your self-confidence.** As I write this, I am aware of the enormity of the task. As someone who has done the work, my relationship with my own boundaries only truly changed when I gained the self-confidence to believe I deserved the respect of others.
- **Where possible, start from the beginning.** Retroactively enforcing boundaries can be difficult, as you have to break learned patterns of behaviour. Try being upfront early on.
- **Be as consistent as you can.** It's important to give others a strong sense of what works for you and what doesn't.
- **Find the language to communicate when your boundaries are crossed.** Get comfortable saying 'no', and try using 'I statements' to express your feelings. An 'I statement' focuses on how you feel and what you need rather than what the other person is or isn't doing. For example:

HOW TO USE I STATEMENTS

I feel .... *when* ....
because ....
What I NEED is ....

What to Do If Someone *Crosses a Boundary*

If someone crosses your boundary, you can:

- **Reiterate the behaviour that you want to receive.** Being clear and confident in communicating the changes you want the other person to make is a big part of enforcing a boundary.
- **Be clear about the consequences of their actions.** For example, you might say, 'I won't attend another client meeting with you until the behaviour is clearly changed.'
- **Remember that boundaries are not about other people, they are about you.** You need to respect your own boundaries in order to encourage other people to respect them too.
- **Understand your tolerance.** You will be aware of the threshold that you have for allowing people to

cross your boundaries. Some people operate on a 'one strike and you're out' policy, others might allow people three chances. Stick to what feels natural for you.

- **Speak to someone.** Whether it's someone at work, a friend, or a therapist, working through the issue verbally with someone with whom you feel safe is important.

If you are dealing with someone who repeatedly crosses your boundaries, things can get difficult. You may decide to accept the behaviour of the other person, and reshape your boundaries accordingly. This might look like spending less time with them, not helping them out when they are in a bind, or limiting what you tell them about your personal life.

And, although this is the hardest part of boundary-setting, there may come a time when you have to face the reality that the person constantly crossing your boundaries does not have a place in your life any more. Distancing yourself from them or ultimately cutting them out completely is a form of reinforcing a more severe boundary to protect yourself.

Think About *Online Boundaries* Too

Are you doomscrolling, looking at people with the body type you want, the job you crave or the handbag you think you'll never be able to afford? If the content is making you feel empowered, excited, motivated and driven, then fabulous. If it's making you feel unhappy, unsuccessful and small, then mute it.

KNOW YOUR NON-NEGOTIABLES

When I interviewed Conna Walker, founder of the hugely successful House of CB, she told me that she had never signed a contract that didn't work for her. She was incredibly matter of fact about the reality of which deals worked for her and which didn't. Her power in negotiating is that she is fundamentally willing to walk away if a deal doesn't serve her. When negotiating at work or in our personal lives, we have been taught that flexibility, compromise and deals that work for everyone are the most desirable. However, this means that we are taught to be willing to weaken our position by giving away some of what we have. While there are instances in which negotiation can be an important component, it is imperative to have worked out your non-negotiables.

Here are some examples of my non-negotiables when pursuing new clients. The answers all need to be 'yes'.

- Do they understand communications?
- Do I believe I can add value?
- Do I want to work with their team?
- Would my team buy, eat, use or wear their brand?
- Are their values (as people) aligned with mine?
- Do they have a viable budget?

There are other things that I can compromise on, but the above are my non-negotiables. This is based on experience and having previously had loose boundaries that led to me and my team feeling unhappy, losing money, losing brain space, dealing with sleepless nights and spending disproportionate amounts of time on tasks that were unfulfilling and didn't make me enough money.

Essentials *and* Luxuries

In working with CEOs around the world, many also talk about the essentials and the luxuries. This can pertain to many decisions you make, but hiring is a good example. Write a list of the most integral requirements for staff at your company.

For example, they need to have:

- a good attitude
- experience

- proximity
- emotional intelligence (EQ)
- a network
- dedication
- communication
- honesty
- professionalism
- initiative
- confidence
- adaptability
- likeability

And they need to be:

- creative
- a team player
- solution-orientated

Your list may look different or similar. The next stage is to rank these qualities from one to ten (or however many you have). The first half of the list make up your essentials. The second half make up your luxuries. When interviewing potential candidates, this process will help you to focus on what is important to you and your organisation, and will create consistency in your hiring process.

In your own personal development, this is also a useful tool for discovering what is important to you. Write a list of things that create an optimal environment for you.

For example:

- strong coffee
- good Wi-Fi
- silence
- being in the office
- being part of a team
- headphones
- supportive peers
- being well rested
- working out
- eating well

Repeat the process above, ranking them in order of importance to identify which are your essentials or non-negotiables, and which are your luxuries. The goal here is to really enhance your self-awareness with regards to setting yourself up to win, and becoming comfortable in communicating that information to others.

A *Final Word* on Boundaries

Remember:

- It's not your responsibility to make other people happy.
- You are not responsible for others' poor decisions, nor is anyone else responsible for your decisions.

- It's not your job to rescue people from their own self-created shitshow.
- You aren't helping others be accountable or set their own boundaries if you never uphold your own.
- You don't need permission from someone else to show up the way you want to in the world.
- Behaviours and feelings are not the same things.
- 'No' is a complete sentence.
- Every decision you make does not require an explanation so others can understand it.
- Life is not about changing other people. It's about showing up as the best version of you, and inspiring others around you to do the same.

CHAPTER 4

Mind(ful)

'Proceed as if success is inevitable.'

ANONYMOUS

If self-development and career progression were a drinking game, 'imposter syndrome' would be the buzz phrase, and you'd immediately be wasted. It's an indulgent, wide-ranging phrase that has been used lazily by entrepreneurs to describe any situation when they've felt out of their depth. Imposter syndrome has had terrible PR and has transitioned from being a retrospective analysis of caution to becoming an excuse for what is ultimately a limiting belief system. In this chapter, we will focus on this phenomenon, considering whether it can actually work in your favour. We'll be exploring mental resilience (if you're a young person looking to do it all, you'll need this). I'll also cover the most important lessons I could wish to impart to you: being big, exploring self-promotion and psycho-cybernetics. This chapter looks at taking accountability for your own progress, and teaches you how to become your very own hype woman.

IMPOSTER SYNDROME

High achievers can often experience imposter syndrome, which manifests as self-doubt in your achievements, ability and intellect. What this means in practical terms is that you feel like you don't belong, or are not worthy of the role you are in, or the responsibility that you have. If you have answered yes to more than two of questions in the list below, it's likely you've experienced imposter syndrome.

Ask yourself the following questions:

- Does your inner voice sound like a broken record asking you why you deserve to be here?
- Is your inner voice a critic, suggesting that you're not capable of providing the right answer?
- Does your self-doubt slow down your decision-making in a helpful way, inviting you to make better decisions?
- Does your self-doubt paralyse you and prevent you from making decisions?
- Do you productively gather constructive feedback with the goal of continuous improvement?
- Do you respond to constructive feedback by scolding yourself for not being perfect?

- Are you unable to trust or communicate with your gut?
- Do you feel stressed, overwhelmed or sad when thinking of progressing in your career?
- Do you often beat yourself up mentally for not being good enough?

Throughout the entirety of my business journey, it seems that every panel, podcast or magazine article I've come across has asked entrepreneurs about their personal experiences of imposter syndrome. Predictably, and often reassuringly, nine times out of ten, the entrepreneur cites that of course they have experienced imposter syndrome, confirming to the audience that no one really believes they know what they are doing, and they are all just making it up every day.

I have two challenges to this:

1. You shouldn't feel imposter syndrome often.
2. Imposter syndrome isn't a bad thing.

The *Four Ps*

Imposter syndrome is a common experience for many women, especially those who are striving to live a smarter and more fulfilling life. Below, we will explore the four main factors that contribute to imposter syndrome, which, according to Clare Josa in her book *Ditching Imposter Syndrome*, are commonly referred to as the four Ps: people-pleasing, perfectionism, paralysis and procrastination. Understanding these aspects will empower you to identify and overcome imposter syndrome and so lead a more confident and successful life.

People-pleasing

People-pleasing is a tendency to prioritise others' opinions or needs over our own. Many women struggle with this, often feeling the need to gain approval and avoid conflict. However, this behaviour can lead to a sense of never being enough, ultimately fuelling imposter syndrome. By recognising the importance of self-care and setting healthy boundaries, you can overcome your people-pleasing tendencies and cultivate a healthier sense of self-worth.

Perfectionism

Perfectionism is a relentless pursuit of flawlessness and unrealistic expectations of one's own performance. Women often fall into this trap due to societal pressures and high personal standards. However, striving for perfection can be exhausting and detrimental to mental wellbeing. By embracing imperfections, setting realistic goals and celebrating achievements, you can break free from the cycle of perfectionism and find greater satisfaction in your accomplishments.

Paralysis

Paralysis refers to a state of being emotionally or mentally stuck, unable to move forward due to fear of failure or being exposed as a fraud. This often manifests as self-doubt and a lack of confidence in your own abilities. Overcoming paralysis involves challenging negative self-beliefs, reframing fear as an opportunity for growth, and taking small steps towards goals. By proactively facing challenges, you can build resilience and regain your sense of agency.

Procrastination
Procrastination is the act of delaying tasks or decisions, often driven by a fear of not meeting expectations. This can be a manifestation of imposter syndrome, as you may feel overwhelmed or unworthy of success. By implementing effective time-management techniques, breaking tasks into manageable steps, and developing a growth mindset, you can combat procrastination and cultivate a productive and fulfilling lifestyle.

By understanding and addressing the four Ps, we can gain the confidence and resilience necessary to thrive in our personal and professional lives without succumbing to burnout or self-doubt.

Imposter Syndrome *Isn't* a Bad Thing

Radical, I know. The reason I wanted to write this book is because I believe that it's not seismic shifts, unrealistic expectations or unthinkable switches that culminate in change. It's the individual inches that add up to the mile. In the Smarter Method, reframing is talked about in relation to many of the changes you are encouraged to make, challenging what you have been led to believe. Imposter syndrome has almost always been considered a negative thing – but is it really? There are qualities often cited when analysing successful people. The first is a belief that you have something to offer the world. The second is a fear of not being good enough. While an eternal and constant feeling that you don't belong, are not worthy or don't have a value relevant to the opportunity is obviously a bad thing, imposter syndrome can also keep you in check.

With this in mind, we'll be exploring ways to combat imposter syndrome – but not eliminate it completely.

> 'Success is most often achieved by those who don't know that failure is inevitable.'
>
> *Coco Chanel*

Dealing with *Imposter Syndrome*

Constantly experiencing imposter syndrome is not a good thing. It's not conducive to long-term success and, frankly, it's exhausting. It becomes increasingly difficult to focus on the task at hand, because so much time is taken up worrying about when it might all come crashing down. The graphic below shares some tips on the best ways to keep imposter syndrome at bay.

MANAGE IMPOSTER SYNDROME

FOCUS ON THE **FACTS**	FIGHT FEELINGS WITH **EVIDENCE**	**KNOW** WHEN TO QUIT
SIT WITH FEELINGS, THEN **RELEASE** THEM	**REFRAME** NEGATIVE THOUGHTS	**ANTICIPATE** FEELINGS
SHARE IT WITH SOMEONE	GET **BETTER**	**LEARN** MORE

Embracing Imposter Syndrome, *Overcoming* Self-doubt and *Thriving*

While I won't deny that imposter syndrome can be a little bitch – it can make us feel like we're not good enough, like we're just faking it – research shows that imposter syndrome can also actually push us to work harder and strive for excellence.

Imposter syndrome was first identified back in 1978, and at the time was mainly thought to affect women in high-achieving careers. And guess what? It still affects a lot of us, especially women. Studies from the University of Salzburg and MIT reveal that about seventy per cent of people have experienced imposter syndrome at some point in their lives.

Now, let me level with you. I've rarely experienced imposter syndrome myself in relation to my work. I've always felt prepared, educated and confident in my expertise. Sure, I've had moments of self-doubt, overwhelmed by the challenges ahead. But I've learned to view those doubts as a reminder to stay on top of my game. In my personal life however – well, that's another story. I've experienced imposter syndrome relating to my ability to be attractive enough to be dated by someone who treats me well, to create a home, and to compile a picture-perfect photo album in line with what society tells us is acceptable. And I really struggled with the idea that in one aspect of my life I could feel so competent, while feeling like a total loser in another. This only exaggerated my public versus private face, and, over time, led to severe anxiety and the fear of being 'found out'.

I have tried very hard to move those two personas closer together. If there are only ever two options – change it or accept it – then I decided to give myself a break. The world tells us how we should look, sound, dress, act and talk. We are bombarded with a constant stream of content, picking out our imperfections and encouraging insecurity. It's no wonder that occasionally we let the negative thoughts in. It wouldn't be realistic to hope for a time when I would never experience any of these feelings. Instead, I wanted to change how I felt about them.

Reframing the idea of imposter syndrome has been key for me. Instead of letting it bring me down, I see it as an opportunity for growth, a chance to question myself and gather more information. It slows down my decision-making process, preventing me from making rash, emotional choices, and keeping me focused on my gut, instinct and logic. As I have discovered, the ability to trust my gut is a key part of the intuition that makes me a good decision-maker.

When you doubt yourself, it opens your eyes to others who doubt themselves. It sparks empathy within you, connecting you with those who have faced similar challenges. When you're willing to question yourself, you become curious and open-minded. You're not afraid to shift your perspective, uncover your strengths and weaknesses, and find better solutions. Dr Valerie Young, author of *The Secret Thoughts of Successful Women: Why Capable People Suffer from the Impostor Syndrome and How to Thrive in Spite of It,* says it best: 'Doubt breeds creativity, which is essential for innovation.'

When you are more open to the idea of shifting your mindset, more open to being wrong, and more open to uncovering the strengths and weaknesses you have, you are more likely to find a better solution in the end rather than getting stuck on your first response.

Another important point is that when we feel like imposters, we tend to compensate by working extra hard or becoming exceptional team players. It's like we're trying to prove ourselves, right? In this way, our experience of imposter syndrome can give us an edge, encouraging us to work smarter, and become solution-orientated and other-orientated.

I know that you're thinking: *WTF is 'other-orientated'?*

Being other-orientated is making the conscious effort to put the thoughts, needs and feelings of others first, without abandoning our own needs in the process.

Tips for Managing *Imposter Syndrome*

- **Context is important.** Tune in to the nuances of each scenario in which you notice your imposter thoughts surface and ask yourself: 'Are these thoughts helpful?' If they are, they will push you in the direction of continuous improvement. If they are not at a healthy level, they will end up sabotaging you. When you learn to appropriately discern when, where and with whom humility is more productive and when, where, and with whom confidence is more helpful, you can slowly learn to dial these capacities up or down according to context, and you will take your leadership skills to the next level.
- **Separate your past image from your current one.** If you have a tendency towards imposter syndrome or imposter thoughts, check in with yourself each year to reassess your competence and ground that assessment in the evidence that supports your actual credibility, not the voice in your head that thinks you

are still a novice. Because confidence can rise faster or slower than your competence and experience, it is a healthy practice to take an honest look at whether or not yours appropriately align.

- **Challenges are opportunities for growth.** Embrace them.
- **Failure isn't the end.** It's a learning experience.
- **Rejection is redirection.**
- **Effort is the path to mastery.** Trying hard is cool.
- **Foster a passion for continuous learning.**
- **Seek and appreciate constructive feedback.**
- **Environment is everything.** Surround yourself with individuals who inspire growth.

MENTAL RESILIENCE

I have worked with a long list of successful people, and they all share a particular trait: mental resilience. Many have had personal and/or professional experiences that have completely untethered them from all that they knew and all that they thought to be real. This trauma heals over time, and the healing leaves us stronger, tougher and more resilient. I'm not talking extremes here – I don't believe stoicism is a progressive way to live, and I believe that empathy, compassion, high EQ and emotional capacity make for exceptional leaders. Many of these qualities are enhanced by enduring extremely trying mental times. There is no easy way around this one. Mental resilience is a key quality in the pursuit of smarter living.

Mental resilience refers to your ability to emotionally process challenges and create thoughtful work-arounds. This is really difficult to do if you feel like a worthless piece of shit and think you're about to be 'found out'. In the rawest sense of the phrase, mental resilience is built from hardship. In the same way that we build muscles in the gym, by challenging our brain, we build resilience. However, our gym goals also rely on the community around us, what we eat, how often we train, the rest days we take, how much water we drink, and setting realistic time frames. The same is applicable for our mental resilience.

There are seven pillars that help you to build mental resilience:

1. self-care
2. self-awareness
3. positive relationships
4. mindfulness
5. purposefulness
6. challenging negative self-beliefs
7. doing things that challenge you (jumping into cold water, pitching to a big client, emailing someone you think might not reply)

Being Big: *Self-Promotion* and *Psycho-Cybernetics*

When I was younger, I wanted to be small. Small physically (something I never actually achieved), small in what I asked for, and small in the space I took up in the world. I thought I should have fewer opinions, get on with things quietly and move slowly. As I learned more and grew up, I realised that the best thing we can do in our lives is be *big*, and now that is something I strive for, take pride in and celebrate. When you adopt an abundant mindset, there is enough space for everyone, no matter how big we are. You might want to be the stage, supporting people, holding people up, you might want to control the spotlight, design the costumes, or direct the play. You might want to be the star. There's room, hunnies.

Self-promotion is intrinsically linked to self-confidence. Often, the way we self-promote actually distracts from our achievements, as we all have different measures of what we feel 'deserves' to be shared. Our currency is 'likes from strangers', and while we understand that what we are sharing with the world is the rose-tinted vision, we still struggle to grasp that other people are doing that too. Instead of taking content with a pinch of salt, we take it verbatim. One of the biggest challenges I see faced by those who seek a smarter life is the pressure to share a constant stream of huge wins: winning an industry award, securing impressive fundraising, hiring a C-suite member of staff, achieving a lucrative exit from a company, being fertile, suiting a bob. The platforms we feed into and the followers that we have create an echo chamber of one-upmanship that makes us feel shitty. The way to tackle this, is to consider two questions:

1. If you didn't share any news on social media, what would be important to you?
2. What holds true value in your life?

Try and answer these questions honestly. I'll show you mine if you show me yours.

1. **If you didn't share any news on social media, what would be important to you?**
   Maintaining movement everyday (ideally Pilates), the happiness of my team at work, delivering results for my clients, buying overpriced London coffee and drinking it lukewarm, meeting new dogs, smelling the pages of a new book, getting a bargain, telling someone I like their outfit, a thunderstorm. (These can help you shape your 'Daily Dos' – see page 180.

2. **What holds true value in your life?**
   Making money to have the freedom to do what I want to, staying connected to perspective, hearing the stories of others, being at peace with putting down a book before the end if I don't like it, talking to my family every day, being physically pain-free.

Not only will your answers to these questions help you to practise gratitude, but they will also reconnect you to your value system and help you understand what you are sharing for you, and what you are sharing for others. Self-promotion shouldn't be about lying online. Self-promotion should be about truly connecting with what makes you happy and fulfilled, and what you are an expert in, and sharing more of that with the world.

What *Is* Psycho-Cybernetics?

> 'No one is a "success" in all areas of their life and no one is a "failure". We all carry around seeds of both. But our habitual actions will carry us more in one direction than the other.'
>
> *Maxwell Maltz*

Psycho-Cybernetics by Maxwell Maltz is a brain-changing book. It was originally written in 1960, with a more modern, up-to-date edition published in 2023. It teaches us about the human self-image, how it's crafted and how it can drastically affect your happiness and success. The book suggests that by changing our self-image, we can change our attitudes and ultimately our behaviour. I am not going to do a deep-dive into this theory, as the book itself is the ultimate storyteller, but I will give you a summary of Maltz's thoughts on how we see ourselves, and how others perceive us – and, of course, how this relates to the Smarter Method.

WTF is my ego, and is it acting for me?

Your ego is your conscious mind, the part of your identity that you consider your 'self'. Self-confidence and ego are two very different concepts. To have confidence is to believe in your own abilities, in yourself. Your ego differs to confidence as it acts out of self-interest. Seeking approval, validation and the limelight, the ego needs to be validated at all costs. The ego is disinclined to accept feedback and can assign meaning where it doesn't exist, attributing motive where there might not be any.

To work out if your ego is in control, consider the following questions:

- Have you ever disliked the idea of someone else succeeding?
- Do you compare yourself to others?
- Do you seek attention for things you didn't do?
- Do you see yourself as better, cleverer or nicer than others?
- Do you like talking about other people's imperfections and flaws?
- Have you ever noticed that you're 'virtue-signalling'?
- Have you ever looked down on someone else for not trying as hard as you?
- Do you set yourself impossible goals and then beat yourself up when you don't reach them?

The ego is closely linked to a scarcity mindset. If you resonate with the above points, I'd hazard a guess that your cup does not runneth over.

Your reactions to the achievements of others are based on your own world view, and the environment in which you find yourself. They are tethered to the demonic mind-fuck that is self-esteem. It's much easier to be happy for someone else who is in a relationship if you don't feel single. It's easier to congratulate someone on their weight loss if you're happy with your own body. At the same time, it's easy to be rude about your friend's pay rise if you feel you're being underpaid. Your reaction to the success of others is a direct mirror of how you feel about yourself. The smarter thing to do is to identify, unpack, control and change your perceptions of the success of others, and you can do this by focusing on your own success. As you move through this book, you will be presented with a number of tasks and suggestions that will help you reconnect with your own goals, as well as the systems and processes that will help you achieve them. As you continue with your own journey, practising gratitude for what you have, focusing your time and energy on your own goals and considering the ways in which you can make your own boat go faster (see page 201), negative thoughts about the success of others will subside.

Glass ceilings or sticky floors?

In storytelling, there are three sides to every story: mine, yours and the truth. Our experiences, realities and make-up create our own unique world view. We see things not as they are, but as we are.

In personal development, despite the many theories, causes, structures and systems, there are always – and only – two choices. You can learn to love the situation you are in, or you can change it. Many of us have experienced decision paralysis, fear of failing or being ridiculed, talking ourselves in and out again of solutions, and outcomes by committee. It can feel impossible to ascend when the ladder is endlessly vertical. One of the greatest challenges we face, is to operate in progressive ways within a system that is outdated and clumsy.

Many people reading this book will be familiar with the glass ceiling analogy. The glass ceiling is essentially an invisible and unacknowledged barrier to advancement in a profession, especially affecting women and people of minorities. In certain industries, the glass ceiling is more profound. However, women all over the world are breaking through this glass ceiling and viewing it as a target rather than a barrier. Here are some examples:

- **Ellen Johnson Sirleaf:** Elected President of Liberia in 2006, making her Africa's first female head of state.
- **Madeha al-Ajroush:** Paved the way for women to drive in Saudi Arabia.
- **Monica McWilliams:** Formed the Northern Ireland Women's Coalition.
- **Mae Jemison:** The first Black woman in space.
- **Stacey Cunningham:** Became president of the New York Stock Exchange in 2018, the first woman to hold that position.

- **Kathryn Bigelow:** Director of films including *Point Break*, *K-19: The Widowmaker* and *Zero Dark Thirty*. Her 2006 film *The Hurt Locker* earned her a spot in history as the first female to win the Oscar for Best Director.
- **Danica Patrick:** Holder of several records in the car-racing world, including being the only woman to place first at the Indy Japan 300, which she accomplished in 2008. At the time of her 2018 retirement, she was (and still remains) the most successful female in Indy racing history.
- **Baroness Swanborough:** In October 1958, she became the first ever woman to take her seat in the House of Lords. Earlier that year, on 30 April, the passing of the Life Peerages Act allowed women to sit in the House of Lords for the first time.
- **Ada Lovelace:** English mathematician who wasn't just the first woman to publish a computer algorithm, but the first person to do it fullstop. Way back in 1840, she wrote what is considered the first algorithm designed for a computing machine.
- **Gertrude Ederle:** Known as the 'Queen of the Waves', on 6 August 1926 she became the first woman to swim across the English Channel, completing the feat in fourteen hours and thirty-four minutes.
- **Ella Fitzgerald:** Jazz singer who made history as the first woman to win a Grammy at the inaugural Grammy awards in 1958.

- **Junko Tabei:** The first woman to reach the summit of Mount Everest, which she achieved in 1975, and the first woman to ascend all Seven Summits by climbing the highest peak on every single continent.
- **Baroness Valerie Amos:** Took her seat in the House of Lords in 1997. She was the first Black woman to do so.
- **Carol Ann Duffy:** Became the first female Poet Laureate of the UK in 2009, nearly 400 years after the role was introduced.

Of course, this analogy can expand. We have the glass cliff, there are rusty rungs, the ladder is vertical, and the list goes on.

The glass cliff refers to the promotion of women during riskier and more challenging times for a company, when the failure rate is higher. Giving them the gift of a proverbial shit sandwich, rather than the perfect picnic. Their failure is then used as an example of why women should not be promoted to these positions in the future, without taking into account the reality of the challenges that they faced.

As we have seen, the Smarter Method asks you to focus on yourself and the impact you can have on your own life, and subsequently the lives of those around you. When it comes to the glass ceiling, the part of this that you can control is not *whether* you break through the glass ceiling – you will. It's about igniting lift-off. And lift-off can be made considerably more difficult by the presence of sticky floors. 'Sticky floors' is used as a metaphor to point to a discriminatory employment pattern that keeps workers, mainly women, in the lower ranks of the job scale, with low mobility and invisible barriers to career advancement.

There is no doubt that there is a huge amount of progress still to be made for women in the workplace. However, it is difficult to dispute that there has ever been a better time in history to be a working woman. We must, as individuals, take accountability for our own actions, and take advantage of what is available to us, in order to continue to work smartly through the infrastructure that we are presented with in our working lives.

THE HYPE WOMAN

As I have explained, in my observation of successful people, it is apparent that they all have a combination of emotions that stem from defiance, not feeling good enough, or a desire to prove someone wrong. The adjustment the Smarter Method asks you to make is to consider pursuing your goals for yourself rather than for others. It is desirable to be driven, to want more, and to believe that you can be smarter in the way you go about it, but it's important to do this for yourself. Success driven by the desire to make others feel less-than comes from a place of scarcity rather than abundance.

The turning point for me was when I changed the way I spoke to myself. Think about the way you talk to yourself. Would you ever consider saying some of the things you say to yourself to your friends? Or to your daughter, or to your colleagues? I actually wrote down and then deleted some of the things I have said to myself in the past, because they were a) unbelievable and b) savage. When I look back now at how I used to speak to myself, I see it as a direct reflection of how unfulfilled I was. I didn't connect with any of the literature that told me to open my heart to the world, or to stare in the mirror and tell myself I was a superstar. I attracted energy that was negative, felt that everything was difficult, moved through things as though they were treacle, couldn't take a compliment, and avoided reflective surfaces. It hadn't even occurred to me that I was basically hate-speaking to myself on a daily basis, because so much of it was happening automatically, and in my own head. This had to change.

In connecting with your own ambitions, desires and challenges, and truly placing yourself at the centre of the process to achieve them, in setting yourself up to win, in adopting an abundant growth mindset, in wanting what is best for you, and in giving life to systems and processes that enable you to achieve your wildest dreams of success, you are connecting with the part of yourself that dares to consider these things are possible.

In a world that requires you so often to consider yourself in the context of others, this method is about placing yourself at the very centre. As you become more confident with this idea, you will be able to more clearly visualise yourself in an achieving role, and feel more connected to your ego in a healthy way. Although there aren't shortcuts, there are hacks. My favourite is the hype woman.

The hype woman isn't just about being nice to yourself. Once, I found myself captivated by a confidence coach whom I heard speaking on a popular podcast. She oozed self-awareness and had an abundance of self-belief. It made me consider what my day-to-day life would look like if I had her in my ear, egging me on, challenging my limiting beliefs and helping to verify my thoughts and ideas. So, I created her. Beyoncé has Sasha Fierce. Call her an alter ego, a ghost, a cartoon, or a coach, but creating your own version of a hype woman is an important part of this method.

Research suggests that speaking about ourselves in the third person can help us remain objective and allow us to consider scenarios that our subconscious might previously have restricted. Essentially, you can trick your brain.

If you are struggling with this concept, start by writing down, somewhere private, the thoughts that currently pass through your head about yourself – all those self-criticisms and doubts. Read them back. Could you imagine reading them out loud to your best friend to motivate her? Could you imagine overlaying them on an image of a mountainous backdrop to create an inspiring and thought-provoking meme? No, of course you couldn't. I couldn't even write mine down in this book because they were so horrifying. Being presented, in black and white, with the sharpness of our own tongues can be sobering. So now, strike through the thought with a line, then replace it with what you'd say to your best friend. Say that to yourself instead. This is a cathartic process and one that helps you to unpick the habits you've formed regarding the way in which you speak to yourself.

Tips for *Being Kinder* to Yourself

- **Don't speak in extremes.** It's very easy to catastrophise when you're anxious and stressed. If a client hands in their notice, this can quickly become: 'All my clients are leaving.' If an item of clothing doesn't fit? 'I'm too fat for my whole wardrobe.' If he doesn't text back? 'I'll be alone forever.' Try and be cognisant of when you are taking an isolated incident and turning it into a generalisation. It can be much harder for us to deal with something challenging if we snowball it into a bunch of other fears that have not yet been realised.
- **Write down the mean things you think about yourself.** Edit them to match what you'd say to your best friend.
- **Acknowledge the thought, but accept that it's not helpful.** Thoughts can be temporary – it's OK to think them, and then move on.
- **Remember that our brains have a negativity bias.** This means that we are literally wired to focus more on negative memories and experiences than neutral or positive ones. You have to make a concerted effort to focus on positive things, and if you are struggling with negative thoughts, that's totally normal.
- **Avoid labels.** Try not to brand yourself as undatable, rubbish at your job, or unfashionable. Isolated

incidents do not have the power to define you and your intentions, or personality.

- **Stop the thought.** Therapists will tell you to use visualisation to picture the thought as an object or thing. In my exploration of this topic, I had to explore feelings connected to shame (haven't we all . . . ?). For some reason, mine was always green, furry and triangular. I practised stopping the thought (or the furry praline Quality Street, according to my vision). At times, I was encouraged to put it into a shredder, turn it into a piñata, or simply throw it out of the window. Giving an identity to the negative thoughts, giving them a shape, helped me to visualise them as something that I could easily get rid of. It gave me an enormous sense of power, and a feeling that I could control the extent to which I looped thoughts and tortured myself about the what-ifs.

Tip: Adopt a *Growth Mindset*

Having a growth mindset means believing that a person's abilities aren't innate but can be improved through effort, learning and persistence. A growth mindset is all about the attitude with which a person faces challenges, how they process failures, and how they adapt and evolve as a result.

CHAPTER 5

Manage

'The key is in not spending time, but in investing it.'

STEPHEN R. COVEY

Understanding where your time goes, how to manage it, and how to make it work for you is a life hack that will transform your routines. In this chapter, I make a strong case for ditching multitasking, encouraging you instead to switch to mono-tasking, a more robust and efficient way to tackle your work. This chapter encourages you to consider how important tasks are, and then eliminate or delegate those that are less important, in order to free up your time so you can accomplish more. You'll learn about how to 'Stop, Start, Continue' habits and patterns that are either working or not working for you, and you'll be introduced to the novelty bias and how it might be impacting the way you work without you realising it. Time- and task-management are incredibly unsexy topics. They're well covered in business books with dusty images from an era none of us were born in. This chapter will simplify your management of this area, helping you achieve long-term success, with the added benefit of streamlining your day and reducing the noise between your ears.

MONO-TASKING

The definition of multitasking is simple: it means to deal with more than one task at the same time. The phrase has been adopted by all sorts of typically high-achieving people, including mothers, entrepreneurs, professionals, and those who identify as 'busy'. Historically, it has been a mark of status to be able to achieve multiple tasks at the same time, and it has also been gendered, with the old adage that 'men can't multitask' becoming a go-to way to claim that men are useless.

However, the fact is that our brains cannot complete multiple tasks at the same time. When we think we are 'multitasking', the tasks are actually being carried out in a sequence, with our attention often returning to the initial task before revisiting a new one so that our brains are rapidly switching between tasks. This constant switching is draining for the brain, tiring us out more quickly. It has a negative effect on our ability to focus, even when we are not multitasking. Studies show that when the brain is constantly switching gears to bounce back and forth between tasks – especially when those tasks are complex and require our active attention – we become less efficient, use up more energy and are more likely to make a mistake. I often think of this task-switching like a metronome. Mesmeric and hypnotic in its rhythmic dance, the pendulum repetitively bounces from side to side – if we were to apply this to our own lives, though, we'd likely flop back and forwards and never have enough time to stop and focus.

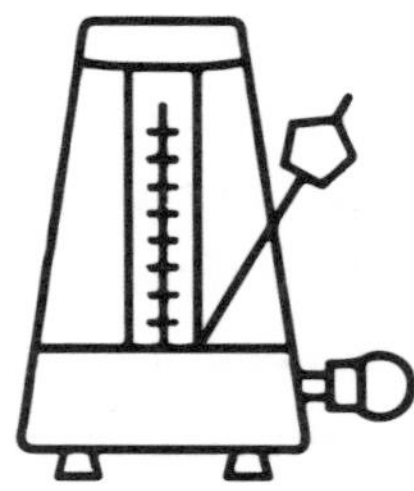

That's right, my friends and sisters who pride themselves on being able 'to do a million things at once': multitasking is a **biological impossibility**. You cannot properly focus on more than one thing at a time. We choose how we spend our time each day; we are the architects of our own productivity. We have a limited cognitive bandwidth, and therefore our current busy cycles of doing everything at once are the opposite of productive. Scientists have shown that habitually multitasking lowers our IQ by ten points. Research has shown that doing more than one task at a time, or switching between tasks, reduces productivity by forty per cent.[1]

There is compelling evidence to support the fact that multitasking doesn't work. However, for many of us, it is a habit that has been baked into our routine, and is difficult to give up. Plus, our lives *are* busy. Tasks don't come at us one by one – they come all at once.

Mono-tasking is a new, focused way to think about moving through your daily workload. Mono-tasking, or single-tasking, is the practice of dedicating yourself to a given task, minimising interruptions and distractions until that one task is complete. You can then move on to the next task using the same approach, and so on and so forth. According to a study by researchers at the University of California, Irvine, it takes an average of twenty-three minutes and fifteen seconds to return to an original task after an interruption. This means that working on one thing, to completion, minimises the between-time where we procrastinate before returning to being productive again. The stress of juggling multiple tasks, as well as the time-wasting and lack of focus, makes multitasking undesirable for high performers. Mono-tasking can save a huge amount of time while also creating more focused work. It also means that tasks are complete and you can mentally move on. Reducing the amount you multitask, or indeed not multitasking at all, will lead to smarter work cycles. You'll be able to create more hyperfocus, to move efficiently through your to-do list, and ensure that you are making your energy stores work for you as effectively as possible.

Ways to *Stop* Multitasking

- Accept that you cannot do more than one thing at one time.

- Separate the urgent from the important (see page 146).
- Be realistic about how long tasks will take.
- Challenge yourself to consider why your level of self-worth comes from your level of productivity.
- Note that a busy life is different to a full life.

Ways to *Start* Mono-tasking

- Choose to only make up to three big decisions per day.
- Track your energy, not your time.
- Use a desk timer to keep accountable with tasks.
- Close all of your tabs, and set yourself up to win by creating an environment with few distractions.
- Run your day in minutes. An eight-hour working day is 480 minutes, and only a third of the total time you have in a twenty-four-hour cycle. You have much more time than you think.

HABIT PAIRING

Habit pairing simply asks you to pair a habit you don't like doing with one you do. The power of the feeling you get from doing the task you do like is greater than the negative feeling you have for the one you don't. As we've seen, the Smarter Method is about making small adjustments, not seismic changes. The Smarter

Method also recognises that success cannot be achieved simply through the omission of things you don't like – almost every story in life will be peppered with good and bad. Instead, we can learn systems and processes that allow us to manage those tasks we don't enjoy in a way that makes them less painful.

I have found habit pairing to be a brilliant way to passively create new habits. Here are some good examples:

- Listening to a podcast while doing the washing-up.
- Calling a friend on a long, boring train ride.
- Watching reality television in the gym.

These don't count as multitasking, as they are tasks that require different parts of your brain – you are not switching from one task to the other, as your hands can wash up while your ears listen to a podcast.

Habit-Pairing Task

- Write down a list of up to five habits that you have previously tried to adopt, or up to five habits you would like to have.
- Link them to your desired identity. For example, you might write, 'Successful people would do this,' or 'A happy/healthy person would do this.'

- Consider the time of day, environment or situation that these habits are usually linked to. For example, washing-up often takes place in the evening.
- Now write a list of habits you find easy and enjoyable. The number of easy habits should be the same as the number of desired habits.
- Match each of these easy habits to one of the desired habits. Do this based on the time of day or the environment in which the habits would usually take place.
- You should now have a clearly paired list of habits, and an understanding of when and where they should take place.
- Continue to rework your list as you go, depending on how easy you find both tasks to complete alongside each other.

URGENT VERSUS IMPORTANT

We touched on this briefly in Chapter 1, but it's an important topic, so let's dive in a little deeper. Working out whether something is urgent or important is a skill. It is difficult to do when you can't see the wood for the trees because – guess what? – everything feels fucking urgent and the goddamn house is on fire.

You might generally make your decisions about the difference between something being urgent and important based on the deadline, asking yourself, 'How long do I have before this is due?', and using the answer to decide what has to be done first.

However, deadlines must work for you, and if you're constantly coming up against issues with completing work within the time frame set, there's either something that needs to change about the way you're working, or the deadlines are unrealistic. The outcome, however, should never be that you just endlessly miss deadlines and are forever branded as a deadline-misser. Pro tip: move the deadline *before* you've missed the deadline.

It's also worth remembering that an approaching deadline generally means a task is urgent – but is it important? Here are some helpful guidelines if you're struggling to work out the difference between urgent and important:

- Define both terms – what is your definition of urgent, and what is your definition of important?
- Does the proximity to the deadline determine how *important* a task is?
- Have you considered the environment you need around you in order to complete the task? The rising panic of not having the tools needed to complete a task can often make a task *feel* more urgent than it really is. (This is an environment check, and we'll discuss it in more detail below.)
- Is the deadline real, or have you set it yourself in order to allow yourself to fail, thus affirming your negative self-belief that you are a deadline-misser?

- Could you prioritise the urgency of a task based on your capacity? For example, what are your energy levels? What's your state of mind? Are you firing at 100 per cent, or is it a sixty per cent kinda day? If so, match the task to where you are at, and make that urgent.
- Speak to someone – reach out to people around you, in the office, on social media. Might someone have a template that can make your life easier?
- Understand your task in the context of the overall goal. What or who are you really holding up if you don't complete the task on time?

As I've explained, we can't multitask. De-prioritising tasks based on your own understanding of your capacity, what you're in the mood for, what environment you need to be in in order excel, and what the ideal set-up is for each task, is something that takes practice. The thing to remember is that not everything is urgent. There's a reason that when you go to A&E, the person with a critical injury is seen before the person who has sprained their finger. Doctors are literally presented with life-and-death decisions, and they consider what is urgent versus what is important and act accordingly.

If you can't get enough of this topic (hard to believe), look up the Eisenhower Matrix, which can help you determine what is urgent, not urgent, important and not important.

WTF is an *Environment Check*?

That's a great question – and thank God you asked it, frankly. An environment check is a simple process that demands that you think about the best possible environment to set you up for success when you are doing hard things. Once you have established what you need to achieve first, it is important to think about the time that it will take, your current mood, and what your set-up needs to be in order for you to succeed. For example:

- I need to work from home today as I can't have any distractions.
- I want to be in the office as I don't want to be by myself.
- I need a coffee.
- I want my heating on and a concentration playlist in the background.
- I need to sit away from my computer and create the plan with a pen.
- I need to remove some of these meetings, as they are draining and no one will care if I reschedule them.
- I am going to blow-dry my hair.
- I will need to stay off social media.
- I will need to put my phone on 'do not disturb' mode.

Eliminate *or* Delegate?

Delegation is one of the most challenging management tools to nail. It depends on myriad connected considerations: how much you trust your team, how aligned your team is with the shared vision, the instructions you give, and your own self-worth in relation to achieving. We often hold on to the tasks we know we can achieve because of the gratifying feeling we get upon completion. However, delegation is important, both for you and your own productivity, and for the growth of your team.

Essentially, there are only three ways to move tasks off your proverbial plate: remove them, get someone else to do them, or create a system that can repeat on autopilot. The skill here is firstly to identify tasks that are either not relevant to, or distracting you from, your core goals. If you can identify that you are spending time and energy on a task that does not 'make the boat go faster' (see page 201), you should find a way to eliminate it. The 'Stop, Start, Continue' process can help you here (see page 153).

The *4Ds* of Time Management

Category	Action	Examples
Do	Work on tasks that only take a few minutes to complete. Quickly accomplishing a series of smaller tasks builds momentum for working on larger projects.	• Answering an email • Returning a phone call • Printing a report
Defer (Delay)	Temporarily pause a task that doesn't need to be handled right away, and schedule when you have the availability.	• New request from a colleague • New project idea
Delegate	Reassign an essential task to someone else.	• Weigh tasks that benefit from your specific expertise vs tasks that deliver the same outcome regardless of who is doing it
Delete (Drop)	Remove unnecessary tasks from your schedule and move on.	• Unproductive meetings • Unnecessary emails

The best way to practise this at work is to understand first where your time is going. You can do this by tracking your time, as we discussed on page 83. In the same way that your banking app can tell you you've spent thirty-five per cent of your money for the month buying coffee, your timesheet can show you where your time is going.

Once you've been tracking your time for a month, look at the reality of your time and consider whether or not this is how you want the next month to look. Think about the following questions:

- Are you spending more than fifty per cent of your time working towards your overall goal?
- Are you spending time contributing to someone else's goal? Perhaps one you won't get any credit for? If so, how much of your time is going to this?
- Are you spending enough time investing in creative pursuits that allow you to feel inspired?
- Are there tasks that you have undertaken this month that someone else could have done? If so, is there a consistent reason?
- What could someone else do in order to give you that time back next month?
- Is there a category you can assign your delegatable time to?
- Can you see any trends or patterns? For example, are you always reaching down and doing the work of a junior member of your team? If yes, is this because you don't want them to get into trouble, because you don't have time to teach them, because they did it wrong (maybe you didn't brief them properly),

because they aren't the right fit for the business but you like them and don't want them to get fired, or because you want to get the attention of your seniors and you work in an organisation that values overachievers? Helping to identify the source of the action is an important part in the way that you set up your next month for working smarter.

Considering these questions will help you to identify the kinds of tasks that you can delegate or eliminate next month in order to have more time to focus on what really matters to you.

The *Stop, Start, Continue* Framework

'Stop, Start, Continue' is a great way to track your progress and hone your actions as you move towards achieving your goals. As we know, self-awareness is an important part of the Smarter Method; it is essential that we have an understanding of our own reality in order to make smarter decisions. Simply put, this exercise helps you gain clarity by considering what you need to do more of, what you can introduce, and what perhaps no longer serves you. I recommend that you revisit this exercise every three months. It is also a very useful tool both in the workplace and in your personal life, and I would suggest it could form part of annual review processes to give people a very strong sense of how they are moving towards their goals, and where their focus ought to be applied. Below is an example table to inspire you.

Goal	Stop	Start	Continue
Lose 10kg	Being mean to myself when I haven't reached my targets.	Meal-prepping.	Going to the gym on the weekend with a friend – it really motivates me.
Get a pay rise	Expecting it to happen just because I asked once.	Asking for direct and clear, regular communication from my line manager to help me with my timeline.	Speaking to others who have already got a pay rise, and asking to hear more about their journeys.
Save for a deposit on a house	Spending spare money on shoes.	Downloading a savings app to automate a savings pot for me.	Listening to podcasts about money and how to save.
Sell more of my product	Assuming everyone else is selling more than me.	Getting into the data and learning more about who I am selling to.	Asking questions of my audience so that I can refine the process and make the marketing more specific.

Here's a blank table for you to fill in:

Goal	Stop	Start	Continue

NOVELTY BIAS

In neuroscience, novelty is 'considered as a variable associated with activity in response to stimulation'.[2] What the fuck does that mean? It means that we are hardwired to be more interested in newness. Novelty bias can work on your fears too – the first time you speak at work in a meeting might be completely daunting and scary, but by the tenth time you're likely far more comfortable.

We spend an average of nearly four hours a day on our phones, and check them up to 155 times per day. Have you ever found yourself scrolling through a TikTok feed, or refreshing your email inbox? The reason why: novelty bias. It also causes chaos for our concentration, because depending on your own novelty bias, it might be easier for something new and shiny to attract you, rather than the task you are already trying to focus on.

It's useful to think about novelty bias when we consider the environment in which we are most productive. Our brains create feel-good memories when we experience something for the first time, providing it is a positive experience. This is known as neophilia, or novelty-seeking. Newness is also linked to increased dopamine.

Novelty-seeking is theoretically driven by the brain's reward system, as the discovery of a novel stimulus reinforces further exploration for novelty.[3]

Studies have found that people with high novelty-seeking tendencies are typically enthusiastic, driven by their accomplishments, and often highly emotionally sensitive.

In any given set of choices, novelty bias encourages us to choose the newest option. This is typically an option that we haven't seen or interacted with before, or even previously considered as a choice. Our brains tell us that newer is better. This can present challenges in decision-making, as our attention is often drawn to new, shiny things. So we can end up making decisions at the expense of rational thinking. Research has found that we might even choose the new option over a previously successful, historical one. As such, we are unwillingly over representing novelty and creating a bias. It is also an absolute bitch for concentration, as our minds start to wander, and we crave something new, even if it's just a page refresh on Instagram.

Novelty bias means anything new and interesting will pique your curiosity. We all have an individual novelty bias threshold. Mine is twenty-three minutes. You can discover yours by simply setting a timer when you begin a specific task, and checking the timer when you notice you are starting to look for distractions.

The reason it's important to understand and engage with novelty bias is it helps us to grasp that we are wired in a certain way that leads us to make the decisions that we do. This doesn't mean you have to fight novelty bias all the time (because that also uses energy); it's about creating environments that work best for you.

Tips for Leaning in to *Novelty Bias*

- Figure out at what point your bias kicks in.
- Remove distractions where possible. Close tabs on your computer, turn off notifications, etc.

- Try to focus on intentional actions rather than subconscious ones.
- Consider your two reactions, emotional and practical.
- Connect with your gut and write down what you're thinking.
- Bring awareness to solutions that have previously worked for you.

HOW OUR PERSPECTIVE ON LIFE SHAPES OUR ACTIONS

Our eagerness to try out new things has a lot to do with how we view our lives in terms of success. In a 2019 study, researchers identified two modes of thinking that people commonly adopt as life perspectives.[4]

- **The 'top-down' approach:** Those who see themselves as having the final say on whether they are successful or not may use the top-down method of thinking. If you find that you'd prefer to examine your own personality traits and intentions as a way to determine your success, then you most likely think using the top-down approach.
- **The 'bottom-up' approach:** You might fall into this category if you view your life as the culmination of your achievements and failures, personal relationships and the impact you've made on the world around you. If you feel as though events and people's opinions

about you are the driving force behind your life, then you might be using the bottom-up approach. With this school of thought, other things (not you) decide whether you are successful.

If you fit into the top-down category, you're probably more likely to seek out new experiences, because your own subjective belief system comes before anything else. In other words, this method of thinking may offer a lot more freedom. If you view yourself and the world around you from the bottom-up perspective, then you're probably more cautious, and hold other's opinions in higher regard. Ultimately, neither viewpoint is better than the other.

It is entirely possible to learn how to better manage your energy and time without making huge changes that set you up to fail. Being clear about what you need in order to succeed, checking in with your environment, energy, the urgency of the task and the relevance of delegation can create meaningful, positive change in the way that you manage the tasks at hand. Being in control and active, rather than believing things are happening to you creates a more intentional approach. If you're still struggling to pivot from negative thoughts that you can't manage your workload, personal life or task lists, try referring to the law of assumption. The law of assumption suggests that your imagination creates your reality. If you can truly imagine your desires and assume you already have what you want, you're far more likely to create that reality for yourself.

- Be intentional with your thoughts as they can affect how you experience the world.
- Repetition is key; this isn't a one-time practice (use 'Stop, Start, Continue').
- Learn how to deprioritise tasks that are less important.
- Start each task with a positive assumption.
- Define your desired outcome.
- Act like the person you want to be.
- Choose to be positive.

CHAPTER 6

Modify

'Whether you think you can or think you can't, you're right.'

HENRY FORD

This chapter is about your ability to reframe things. It provides alternative viewpoints to learned habits and interpretations. The Smarter Method teaches you how to make small adjustments over time, rather than seismic changes. Modifying the way you've always done things, reframing decision-making and what you believe to be equilibrium, and understanding why maintenance of environment is critical to success is captured in bite-sized bits below.

REFRAMING DECISION-MAKING

Facts *and* Feelings

When we are faced with a decision, there are always two reactions: the emotional and the practical or logical. Our emotional reaction is what we *feel*, such as excitement, anger or anticipation. Our logical reaction is usually what we *think*, and this often leads to an action, such as firing someone or hugging someone. I realised on my own journey that I had been asked many times to eliminate perceived negativity from my thinking patterns, but now I know that this is not the solution. The solution is to understand where that negativity comes from, why we feel it and whether it is part of an emotional or logical response.

Have you ever been so enraged that you've written your entire memoir in a WhatsApp message, pressed send and had to hover over the screen until it's been read and your victim at the other end starts typing? Praise be to WhatsApp for allowing us to delete such absolute garbage. The emotional driver comes first, typing second. Good decision-makers have the capacity to make the emotional part of the reaction smaller, or secondary, to the logical one.

Reframing is about making micro changes to the way you absorb information and understanding that you have a huge amount of control over the possible outcomes.

The problem with these two reactions – emotional and logical – is that things can become confusing when we consider the gut–brain relationship. We talked earlier about the importance of 'trusting your gut', but that doesn't mean that your gut instinct is an emotional reaction. Our brains have a muscle memory that alerts us to the potential outcome of various situations, and advises us regarding the best course of action. If you're an entrepreneur reading this, you will no doubt remember occasions when you've absolutely kicked yourself for knowing in your gut what the outcome would be, and yet willingly sleepwalking into a situation that now causes problems. 'I knew I should have fired them sooner!' you cry. Why didn't you? If you knew in your gut that the situation wasn't right, why didn't you take action? Did it need to be more severe, more uncomfortable?

Logic:

- **Requires emotion** – Logic cannot always be completed without emotion, especially with regards to decisions that affect life satisfaction. After all, relationships, jobs and other major decisions are not always straightforward. For example, logically, a partner may look great on paper but they do not create feelings of love and excitement. If so, they may not be the right partner.
- **Requires energy** – Logic isn't always a simple process. The amount of mental and physical energy that goes into a logical decision may be more than the time and attention you have allowed. Coming to a logical conclusion quickly can be very difficult.

Emotions

- **Can lie** – How you feel may not actually be what is best for you or what your heart really wants. For example, many former couples – after they break up – feel like they miss their relationship. Some may even give in and get back together. But this can be a mistake, as missing someone (an emotion) is common after any relationship, simply because a part of your life has changed.
- **May be irrational** – By default, emotions aren't controlled by logic. Thus, you can have emotions that are completely irrational given the situation. Anxiety and depression are examples of extreme versions of how this can manifest.

In many ways, logic is better than emotion. The more critically and objectively you can think about a decision before you make it, the more likely it is that you will come to the decision that is best for you. The less you are driven only by emotion and instinct, the fewer impulsive or irrational decisions you should make.

That doesn't mean that you should be without emotion, however. Confusing, isn't it? Emotion still plays a significant role in decision-making, including logical decision-making. There is a natural give and take that exists here, and many of these situations are not absolute. Remember, we aren't looking for absolutes, we are looking for good-enoughs.

Pros *and* Cons

Through the Smarter Method, I am encouraging you to modify what you already know; we hold so much information already, and our brains process so much each day. Much of what you are recalling is already learned – it's about considering how you could better call on and apply the knowledge that you already have. While you are not being encouraged to unlearn previous teachings, you are asked to reframe some of what you already know.

Have you ever struggled to make a big decision, despite the list of reasons to decide one way appearing to totally outweigh the other? Philosopher Ruth Chang delivered a TED Talk[1] about how to make hard choices in which she presented a powerful framework for shaping who we are and how we make decisions. The talk first aired in 2014, but the message is still relevant today. The key takeaway is that we need to challenge the idea of how we confront difficult decisions. We are used to writing a list of pros and cons. Then we might decide that, on balance, there are more cons, and so the decision we make is not to pursue the opportunity. The problem with this is that emotional capacity is not numerically defined. The items on our list carry different value based on a broader range of considerations.

Imagine you're offered a new job, for example, and you decide to write a list of pros and cons to help you choose whether to accept it. You might write:

Pros

- more money

- more flexibility
- better hours
- free lunch
- gym on site

Cons

- located far away from home/family

Here, the pros list is longer, but if it's important to you to be near your family, then the value of the con is greater. In working smarter, try switching out the pros and cons lists, and replace them with pros and cons pies. These pie charts force you to consider the size of each slice (or item on your list), based on importance. You can then work out clearly and visually the weighting of each pro and con. This helps you work out the actual value of each item, rather than point nominally accruing one point.

How to *Make Decisions* Based on Your Values

- Connect with your values. Write down what is important to you. Use the visualisation tools on page 59 to encourage a visual picture of what you want your life to look like.

- Separate your values into pillars: work, romantic relationships, financial, health, friendships and family. This helps you label and prioritise them.
- Play out how different realities will make you feel.
- Give yourself space. We are so often influenced by the world around us. Ensure that you are creating a calm and safe space for yourself to really, truly connect with what is important to you.
- Communicate with other people who have experiences that you feel mirror the ones you want to create. Listening to stories of those who are ahead of you in age, accomplishment or life can inspire you.
- Connect with your logical and emotional responses to possible outcomes.

EQUILIBRIUM – IT'S NOT FIFTY-FIFTY

On page 74, I explained that you don't need to be 100 per cent sure about anything. I also believe that equilibrium is not fifty-fifty. Equilibrium doesn't actually mean that everything is perfectly even. It just means that it all has to add up to 100.

My least favourite adage in the world is when people tell you that you can only have two things that are good at the same time in the triangle of life, work and family. Think about that for just one second. We have a colloquialism that has infiltrated our advice-giving conversations that tells you that it's effectively written that one part of your life must be shitty if the other two are good. And guess what? That paradigm is based on equilibrium being fifty-fifty – it's almost as if we cannot compute thirds.

Tips for *Reframing* Your Concept of Balance

- Try to define what balance means to you. When you feel at your most content, what is happening in your own life and the world around you that helps you to reach this state?
- Where is your desire for fifty-fifty coming from? Does it come truthfully from your own gut, from trusting yourself, or from listening to those around you?
- Draw a circle on a page. Cut it in half. Can you fit all the facets of your life into those two halves, or do you need more segments?
- Listen to yourself. If the total has to make 100, and you're giving sixty to work, you've got forty left. Don't overcommit when you know what is available to you.

THE FISH TANK

The fish tank is a great way to think about the Smarter Method as an ongoing commitment. As with any practice, our success comes from what we repeatedly do. Whether you choose to call it manifesting, hyperfocus, maintenance, hygiene, discipline, practice or habit, it's ultimately all the same thing.

The fish tank is a way of me sharing a lesson that I learned, at huge emotional and financial cost, through hiring my first COO. Spoiler alert, it didn't work out. With hindsight offering twenty-twenty vision, there were a number of reasons why this went wrong. The most obvious was that this person was not a COO who had grown a company. They were a COO who had operated in a company of the size I wanted to be, rather than a COO who was part of the journey of that growth. Cool, you're thinking, but why are we talking about a fish tank? It's a great point, and one I am glad you have raised.

Many people make the mistake of creating systems and processes and expecting, wanting or hoping that they will be implemented perfectly. The reality is that you can create the most wonderfully intended, tried and tested, and seemingly engaged-with processes, but without hygiene, they will always fail.

The reason for my COO failure was that the person creating the processes, in an attempt to make the business more streamlined and efficient, was ultimately too far away from the reality of how those processes ran day to day in the business. The processes were theoretically sound, but in practice, they crumbled. Many of us are well-intentioned, and perhaps even extreme, in the way that we initially commit to change, tasks or new practices. The size of the commitment often correlates to our ego and our sense of achievement. However, it is often the small practices carried out day to day that ultimately compound to create real, lasting change. You can have the most expensive, fabulous fish tank in the pet shop, with all the bells and whistles, different lighting settings, fake coral, colourful stones and a jazzy arch for your prime-bred, overpriced fish to swim through under your expectant gaze. However, if you don't feed the fish, if you don't clean the tank, if you don't monitor the filtration or pay your electricity bill, the fish will always die. The environment you create for yourself must be taken care of as basic hygiene, or it will destroy everything inside it.

Responsible, Accountable, Consulted *and* Informed (RACI)

As your friend, I'll be honest with you. On the face of it, this is the most boring section of this chapter, and possibly even the entire book. However, it is useful enough to be included, so I would encourage you to read on. This is a brilliant – if slightly dry – structure to use to modify your relationship with productivity, and to enhance your ability to both delegate and hold accountable those to whom you delegate.

RACI (pronounced ray-see) is a responsibility-assignment matrix. The four categories are: responsible, accountable, consulted and informed. They refer to the specifics of responsibility in any given task, and are essential for delegation. When I was growing up, my dad impressed upon me that the success of any mission was based on the instructions given. What I believe he was trying to communicate was that if you're the one giving the directions, the buck stops with you. In a management scenario, when we're delegating to team members or indeed dividing up your own tasks, the idea of project management sounds archaic, uncreative and incompatible with the verbiage we use online and in real life. What is relevant – and important – in the context of managing your time and your activity is to learn how to understand what needs your time, when and where. RACI is a great tool to help you to work out where your energy needs to go.

This is how each of the four components of RACI are defined:

- **Responsible:** Someone who is directly responsible for successfully completing a project task.
- **Accountable:** The person with final authority over the successful completion of the specific task or deliverable.
- **Consulted:** Someone with unique insights whom the team will consult.
- **Informed:** Someone who isn't directly involved, but should be kept up to speed.

The goal of the RACI model is to bring structure and clarity regarding the roles that stakeholders play within a project. This responsibility-assignment matrix instils confidence in each responsible person because they know what they are doing.

RACI provides a concrete and intentional framework to manage all relationships appropriately, from start to finish. Mapping out all responsibilities from the beginning is an excellent way to avoid miscalculations and blunders that could cost you precious time and money.

WHAT IS A RACI MATRIX?

R	**RESPONSIBLE** Individual or individuals who are directly involved in doing the work and completing the task.
A	**ACCOUNTABLE** An individual or group who is ultimately responsible for making sure that the work is completed and meets all the project objectives.
C	**CONSULTED** The people or stakeholders who should be consulted and sought inputs and feedback from, before commencing a task or the project.
I	**INFORMED** Individuals who need to be informed about the progress of the project and what is happening in the project execution.

RACI *Tips*

- Use the technology available online to help you build these charts.
- Bring people on the journey with you. Encourage them to see how this process works for them, and ultimately makes their lives easier.

- Make only one person accountable per task or deliverable.
- Allow only one responsibility type per person. If you don't follow this, the RACI matrix will be more confusing than helpful.
- The accountable person needs to have the authority to help finish the task.
- Only the responsible and accountable roles are mandatory for every task. Not every task is complex enough to need outside input or warrant informing anyone else.
- Prioritise effective communication with the consulting person.
- Always keep all stakeholders informed. Even the lowest level needs to know about updates and changes to the project.
- Tell it like it is. This isn't particularly sexy, but, when used effectively, it does work.

CHAPTER 7

Marketing

'Victory has 100 fathers and defeat is an orphan.'

JOHN KENNEDY

I strongly believe that the way you market yourself can have either exponentially positive or negative ramifications on your life. In this chapter, we will explore the power of personal branding, why you've been doing vision boards all wrong, how to set beneficial 'daily dos', and how to build systems that will enable you to achieve the goals you have set for yourself. An ability to understand personal branding, how you frame failure, and consider the smoke and mirrors present in the way that others market themselves, is consistently shown to be a skill that many successful entrepreneurs and productivity pros have mastered. I will also share the idea of 'going ghost' – what is it, and when and why to do it.

A crucial point we will be considering in this chapter revisits one of the three questions I asked in the introduction: Why do you try to prove your value to others, and how much time do you spend doing it?

The first thing we must do is to explore the idea that busyness relates to value. We often overschedule ourselves, keeping busy and talking about being busy in order to feel important, needed, celebrated and envied. Being super busy has become associated with success for many, although busyness rarely correlates to real value. We are oversaturated with content that tells us the most successful people we know are also the busiest.

It's a difficult web to untangle. Much of our upbringing is focused on succeeding, doing more, participating in sports, seeing the world, reading and being well rounded. Much of what we experience online has told us consistently and repeatedly that content is king, likes equate to value and that there is meaning in the feedback we get from imaginary people behind a screen. Many of us are addicted to social media, and it's no wonder. The apps and algorithms are specifically designed to keep us hooked, wanting more and feeding into the system. Research connected to mental health and social media is well covered by those much more qualified than me.

In this chapter, I want to help you challenge the architecture you have previously built around practices relating to productivity, and the perception of yourself that you put out into the world. We will be exploring how much of our activity is driven by how we want to be perceived, rather than how valuable the work we are doing actually is.

When I started my business at twenty-two, I thought I was

Gordon Gekko. I had business cards printed (how terribly unsustainable of me), I spoke loudly on the phone when there were people nearby, and I would often stay late at work, even if I was just watching television on my laptop, because I thought people would respect me more. I'm generally unsure who these people were, but they seemed to have a grip on me. The important thing to note here is that running a start-up or being an ambitious person comes with graft that is impossible to avoid. I'm not talking about side-stepping the work, I'm talking about removing things that don't tie in to your objective value, and ensuring that you ringfence your time to avoid burnout. Much of the useless time I was spending 'working' was, in fact, productivity theatre.

WHAT IS PRODUCTIVITY THEATRE?

Productivity theatre is a phenomenon that is all about performative work that gives off the appearance of being busy, rather than work that creates actual value. According to a new survey from workforce analytics company Visier,[2] eighty-three per cent of respondents said that they'd engaged in performative work in the past twelve months, while forty-three per cent admitted to spending more than ten hours a week doing so (that's more than one-fifth of the traditional working week).

So what are these time-sapping but not particularly useful tasks that we are using to perform our productivity? If the list below resonates with you, then, spoiler alert, you're a productivity thespian.

- responding to emails or Slack messages as quickly as possible
- keeping laptop screens awake even when you're not actually there
- leaving your email, WhatsApp or Slack with tens of unread messages
- red-lining time blocks in your diary so everyone knows you are busy
- sticking Post-it notes all over your screen that mean nothing
- setting your Slack to 'busy' when you're not
- drawing attention to your working lunch, when you're mainly just having lunch
- raising the volume of your voice to be deliberately overheard
- always carrying a book but never reading it
- responding automatically with, 'I'm so busy' when someone asks how you are
- deleting Instagram posts when they don't have a satisfactory number of likes

Our obsession with performative work might stem from the fact that the dialogue around the working day has changed significantly in the last five years. The pandemic sparked discussions around hybrid and remote working; now the concept of the four-day week is slowly becoming more widespread, and an endless cycle of workplace behavioural buzzwords like 'quiet quitting' have pushed conversations about work to the top of the cultural agenda. This has intersected with an explosion of marketed 'showing off' online, such as TikTok videos showcasing productivity hacks or chronicling a perfect day in the life. The mark of success has become how much you can do. It's a 'more is more' mentality.

Perhaps the biggest factor in the rise of productivity theatre, though, is economic uncertainty. Visier's survey found that 'a general fear of job security has made employees want to appear more valuable to their manager and colleagues', according to the company's EMEA North director Ben Harris. With potential redundancies looming, workers are 'feeling the pressure to "impress" leadership and "prove" their overall ability in order to counter the perceived threat of job loss', according to Leeson Medhurst, Head of Strategy at workplace consultancy Peldon Rose. This often results in 'a bigger rise in physical attendance' – aka presenteeism – as many senior leaders still 'feel that visibility of colleagues equals productivity, and that absenteeism is indicative of low performance'.

How to Put a Stop to *Productivity Theatre*

- Highlight three key tasks to complete that day, rather than judging productivity on the length of your to-do list.

- Be strict and pragmatic with your time. When you're off, you're off. Learn how to set boundaries.
- Be present in the parts of your day you choose to give attention to, rather than always thinking about the next thing.
- Run your day in minutes, not hours.
- Track energy, not time.
- Be critical with the tasks you are doing and how you are presenting them back to the business or your online audience. Ask yourself whether it's for them or for you.
- Try not to use the phrase 'I'm so busy' for a whole week.

VISION BOARDS

In addition to the way you market yourself to others, it's important that you also create a clear vision for yourself, and very much bring yourself on the journey. We've already talked about visualisation (see page 56) and the need to 'see it to believe it'. Now I'd like to introduce you to a new way of thinking about creating the life that you want by using vision boards, but with a twist.

A vision board is a collage of images, pictures and/or affirmations that represent your dreams and desires, designed to serve as a source of inspiration and motivation. A collection of visions of what you want to see in your future.

Of course, there is something reassuring about seducing yourself with candles and creating a ritual where you write down your wildest dreams and desires. There are amazing apps, struggling stationery shops and online tutorials that make this practice easy, fun and accessible. There are a few issues with this approach, however: namely, that it isn't setting us up to win. While it is important to have bigger, long-term goals to tether you to your sense of belonging and purpose, this sort of visualisation can promote inaction. I believe in plans, habits, repetition and consistency. Our goals are achieved by the sum of all that we do in preparation for them; turning up to practice is essential if we want to win on game day.

Imagine your goal is to make a million pounds. That is an enormous number and a huge goal. Why defer the moment when you are able to celebrate your achievement and being on the path to glory? Why not create a plan to make £1,000 first? Then repeat it – one thousand times. In his book *Atomic Habits*, James Clear explains:

> Achieving a goal only changes your life for the moment. That's the counterintuitive thing about improvement. We think we need to change our results, but the results are not the problem. What we really need to change are the systems that cause those results. When you solve problems at the results level, you only solve them temporarily. In order to

improve for good, you need to solve problems at the systems level. Fix the inputs and the outputs will fix themselves.

Use the example of tidying your room. You tidy your room, and it's tidy. But if you're a total slob and haven't changed the behaviour that made it untidy in the first place, it will soon become messy again.

Goal setting suffers from a serious case of victor bias. We concentrate on the people who end up winning – the victors – and mistakenly assume that ambitious goals led to their success while overlooking all of the people who had the same objective but didn't succeed. We hear so often about the burning aspiration and desire from the winner in their pursuit of victory, and therefore assume that those who didn't win were not as ambitious, or in some way wanted the prize less.

Every Olympian wants to win a gold medal. Every candidate wants to get the job. Every entrepreneur wants a lucrative exit. Every mother wants a healthy baby. If successful and unsuccessful people share the same goals, then the goal cannot be what differentiates the winners from the losers.

Winner or loser, the goals remain the same, it is the system put in place that is the reason they succeed.

It wasn't the goal of creating a billion-dollar brand that propelled Sara Blakely, the creator of Spanx, into the entrepreneurial hall of fame when she gained investors such as Oprah Winfrey and Reese Witherspoon. Presumably, her desire for global success had been there throughout the twenty years for which the brand had existed. The goal had always been there. It was only when she implemented a system of continuous small improvements that she achieved a different outcome.

All professional athletes want to win gold. All popstars want to reach number one. No one ambitious strives for second. The reason some miss out on the title is due to the incremental plan in place that shapes their day to day. As I was told when playing hockey in Canada: 'You win trophies in practice, you collect them on match day.'

As a new way of thinking about visualisation and the system I needed to put into place to reach a goal, I started what I call 'the Daily Dos'. Consider traditional vision boards goals, and the Daily Dos a system for reaching them.

What Are the *Daily Dos*?

The Daily Dos are a micro vision board: a shifter and shaper of what you actually want your day-to-day life to look, feel, smell, taste and be like. It's great to have huge goals, but not at any cost. Sprinting into burnout due to the pressure of your looming goals isn't the way to living smarter. Instead, try and think about what your vision looks like day to day. I have included mine below as an example. What is important to me, day to day, is:

- movement (being able to move my body)
- learning (being able to steal some time to educate myself)

- showing up to work and doing a job that I love
- listening to a podcast
- laughing
- drinking a delicious, overpriced coffee
- eating at least one cooked/prepared meal at home
- having a good (enough) bedtime routine (and a bath!)

The idea with the Daily Dos, is that you are committing to a system, a daily routine, a repetitive vision of how you want your day-to-day life to be. While it is important to have bigger goals, you won't reach them unless you have an accumulation of habits that stack up to help you reach those goals. Use your traditional vision board to set a direction. Use the Daily Dos to steer the boat.

Reframing Tip

Rather than considering what kind of success we want, we should ask, 'What kind of pain do I want?' What Mark Manson, author of *The Life Changing Magic of Not Giving a F*ck*, realised is that having a goal is the easy part. I'd love to lose 10kg, write a best-selling book, and exit my company for millions. The real challenge is not determining if you *want* the result, but if you are willing to accept the sacrifices required to achieve your goal.

Do you want the lifestyle that comes with your quest? Do you want the boring and ugly process that comes before the exciting and glamorous outcome?

When it comes to my own journey, I have found that being too focused on the bigger vision can actually be counterproductive. For me, it created a yo-yo effect, where I seemed to bounce between goals, often missing the point. Once you reach the end goal – releasing the book, floating the company, raising money, losing the weight – the goal is no longer there to provide motivation. So what do you do next? You set new goals. Hence the yo-yo. This is often where people find themselves reverting to old habits once they have achieved a goal – or, indeed, setting an enormous, difficult goal, because the bigger the goal, the more likely you are to kick yourself into motivated action.

The purpose of setting goals is to win the game. The purpose of building systems is to continue playing the game. True long-term thinking is goalless thinking. It's not about any single accomplishment. It is about the cycle of endless refinement and continuous improvement. Ultimately, it is your commitment to the process that will determine your progress.

Be mindful – vision boards can negatively impact your happiness. Big goals create an 'either/or' conflict: either you achieve your goal and are successful, or you fail and are a disappointment.

YOUR PERSONAL BRAND

The way you market yourself dictates how others choose to interact with you. Having clarity on your own personal brand ensures that you are refining others' understanding of how to work with you – for example, when and where to contact you. As a young business owner, I felt that I had to reply to every email, to give everyone time, and I frequently found myself in meetings that could have been an email. While I do believe it's important to expose yourself to multiple opinions and opportunities, as you become more accomplished and busier, this isn't a smart way to work. It's important to be clear with people about the kinds of opportunities that will pique your interest. Many of us feel we need to be open to everything, to not miss a trick, and it's common to feel that having a busy inbox, LinkedIn page or calendar is conducive to progress. This is not the case. Productivity is not frequency.

Many of the entrepreneurs I work with are hugely inspired by the world around them. They are thinking about the day they are having right now, as well as their five- and ten-year visions. They are constantly iterating, moderating, changing and streamlining their ideas, discarding some and including others, in order to create the best offering possible. This busyness can be hard to quieten, and is so often essential to bright brains battling for their idea to win. When I media-train many of these CEOs, I ask them to consider purity of message – what is the one thing they are hoping to land? Take iconic brand Nike, which needs no introduction. Their message is clear: 'If you have a body, you are an athlete.' They don't tell you: 'We have trainers and socks, and options for modest dressing, and diverse mannequins, and running shoes, and we sponsor athletes.' The brand communicates clearly and simply that they cater to athletes, and that if you have a body, you are one, and so you'll find a product that suits you. Purity of message is important.

Social media gives us a 'can't live with it, can't live without it' dichotomy. It doesn't have to be negative. You are your own influencer. You choose what to look at, what to consume, and what to put out in the world. It's very easy to change the algorithms from competitors, businesses you weren't hired by and stockists who didn't buy your product, to inspiring entrepreneurs, nature, laughter and motivation by deliberately interacting with the content you want to see more of and muting the posts that don't serve you.

How to *Define* Your Personal Brand

- Refine your niche. What are you asking people to come to you for?
- Can you introduce yourself in fifteen seconds or less?
- What areas of life do you gravitate towards?
- What three words come to mind when someone asks what your talents are?
- Use social media as a marketing tool, and assume everyone else is doing the same.
- Hone your expertise. Read, write, get a mentor,

explore, reach out to people, use LinkedIn, sign up to newsletters, start a WhatsApp group.

- Find your audience – who is it that you want contacting you?
- Practise abundance. As we know, there is enough room for everyone. Share what you have learned and help others on their journey.
- Audit your influence. Think about what you are consuming, and whether it aligns with your personal branding goals.

Becoming media trained is marketing speak for knowing what you want to communicate, how and to whom. The goal here is to be able to:

- develop incisive and accessible media messages to communicate a story
- use keywords to add impact to the story, and quotes to inject personality
- structure a clear point of view and deploy memorable facts and context
- explain complex issues in a simple way to TV, radio and print journalists
- prepare quickly and effectively for interviews and press conferences
- anticipate scepticism and 'bridge' away from difficult questions
- handle nerves, tough questions and difficult interviewers

You can also think about how you might answer these questions:

- How can people take what they have learned from your method/skillset and implement this into their lives?
- Why is your message important?
- Can you tell me more about your approach to your chosen category?
- What are your predictions for the future of your industry?
- What do you want me to know about you?
- Think about how this can apply to your life. People treat you how you allow them to treat you.

THE ARENA VERSUS THE STANDS

Brené Brown is an extraordinary woman who captured the imagination of the world by speaking candidly about her many years of research into and insights around vulnerability and shame. Her brilliant book *Daring Greatly* was inspired by 'The Man in the Arena' speech given by President Theodore Roosevelt. She speaks specifically about the opinion of those in the stands, and those in the arena. If you're reading this book, you're ambitious, busy and tired, so I won't tell you to go and read Brené Brown immediately, but I would encourage you to connect with her teachings in some capacity.

Those who criticise you are rarely doing better than you. It is incredibly easy to throw shade, produce a catty comment, reduce a woman's success when ringing the bell to her having a rich husband, suggest motherhood is easier with her nanny, or suggest a naturally high metabolism keeps her lean. Our immediate reactions tell us much more about ourselves than the person they are aimed at. Connecting with that uncomfortable truth is a way of creating accountability for yourself, and you can then choose to direct that thought towards growth.

For example, when your friend gets a pay rise, and your instant reaction is to feel unimportant and poor, consider why you feel like that. What light has your friend's announcement shed on your own personal situation?

- Are you underpaid for your role?
- Are you jealous of your friend earning more money?
- Are you annoyed with yourself that you didn't negotiate with your employer when you took your job?
- Have you not yet had the courage to ask for the pay rise you feel you deserve?
- Are you unhappy in a role that doesn't value you? Do you need to look for a new job?
- Is your value system misaligned with the one that exists at the business you work for?

You can lean on the Smarter Method tools here, by separating your initial emotional reaction from your secondary, intentional and action-focused response. It's absolutely fine to have both reactions, just remember that your situation is unlikely to change if you aren't willing to do anything about it.

When Brené Brown educated us all about the stands and the arena, she was encouraging us to choose an alignment. The saying goes that you shouldn't accept criticism from someone from whom you wouldn't take advice. As you continue along your ambitious journey, you need to make a decision. Are you sitting in the stands? Sure, it's much easier: you're part of a crowd, you get a beer and a hotdog. You can be late and no one will mind. You can wear whatever you want. You can sing songs with your friends and go to the bathroom whenever you like. The alternative is that you play on the pitch. It's harder. The pressure can, at times, be overwhelming. Dreams are made and lost on the pitch. You will work late, early and on weekends. You'll be criticised by people you will never even meet. If you're injured, you'll be rehabilitated. If you're off your game, you might start on the bench. But the bench isn't in the stands. The people who choose the stands don't get to hold up the trophy, or bow for the medal. It's easy to criticise when you're sitting in the stands. But if you choose to play on the pitch, think very carefully about whether or not those are the opinions you want to replay in your head once the roar of the crowd quietens. Feedback and criticism aren't automatically fact. You have a choice about which part of it you decide to use to be inspired by and evolve from. You also have a choice about which part of it you discard.

GOING GHOST

It is useful to share our wins with the people who matter to us. And sometimes, frankly, we feel satisfaction when sharing our wins with those who didn't believe in, want or encourage our success. It's natural to want to prove the naysayers wrong, and to share our accomplishments. The grey area exists when you feel as though your need for success is geared towards the approval of others – for example, if you think something is a bigger achievement because more people liked it on social media, or if you are likely to have your opinion altered, going against your gut, because of the influence of those around you. The Smarter Method encourages you to connect with your gut, your sense of self, and your ability to be brave in the face of challenges. Remember that courage is contagious.

I have found it very difficult to create boundaries with social media, and all the chatter about it can actually make it even noisier than it needs to be. Following a very challenging year in my twenties, I came off social media for seven months. It wasn't even difficult to do, as I was so desensitised and numb to everything. People thought I had died – it was all quite dramatic. The best thing about 'going ghost' in this fashion was that I truly reconnected with what was important to me – something I had totally lost sight of. I genuinely wasn't sure what was real and what was not. I had stopped being present, as I was concerned with capturing every experience through my phone.

I am aware that for many people, this isn't a practical way to exist. We use social media to stay connected, feel inspired, learn, like, share and shout. However, taking time away from the online echo chamber and rooting yourself firmly in your own real life is a crucial part of working smarter. It helps you work out what is just noise. What your real feelings are. What you miss. Who contacts you. How to meaningfully fill your time. How to take fewer photos, so you live in the present and not for the future memory or meme. Much of the noise we experience online is self-inflicted – it's a visual and audio assault on our senses. As ever, we have a huge amount of control over how we manage this. To remove yourself from the fantasy fuckfest that is algorithmic annihilation is to care about your wellbeing and commit to a smarter way of doing things. In order that we might stand a chance of avoiding burnout, it's essential that we know when to turn the volume dial down. When it all gets too loud, going ghost (even for seventy-two hours) can help reset your brain.

Tips *for* Going Ghost

- Don't tell people about it. You don't need to court attention by announcing to everyone that you are going offline.
- The action must be directed by the intention to

nourish yourself and seek quiet. This is not about attention-seeking.

- Don't be a fool. Don't shut down all communication in a way that will create panic amongst those who care for you.
- See the time as a gift to you, from you, to practise stillness.
- Enjoy not having to report all that you do in a day to your faceless followers online.
- Commit across platforms: LinkedIn, Snapchat, TikTok and Instagram.

CHAPTER 8

Mastery

'If you evaluate your productivity by how busy you are, you're using a losing measurement.'

KEITH WEBB

An incredibly powerful piece of advice I received in my twenties is that life is not about eliminating all the parts that are uncomfortable, or cause tension, excitement, fear of the unknown or doubt. Rather, it is about the mastery of them. In this chapter, we will unpack the ideology to which many of us have subscribed: namely, that exhaustion is a measure of success. This chapter will help you to discover how much of your busyness is self-generated, why taking on too much at any given time is a recipe for failure, and how you can use the eight and two theory. We will look at reframing, as well as going into more detail around scarcity and abundance. You'll learn why things are not supposed to be hard forever, and how it will get easier, the more you learn, grow and implement all that you have been taught.

So: here's the tea. Piping hot, just for you. You aren't as busy as you think. * *Pause for audible gasps.**

You've been told that more is more, and that impressive people never have any time, are always doing something, are exhausted, are on the brink of or in the midst of burnout, and are gasping for air. This is an ideology to which I, too, subscribed for many years. I would stay late in the office because I thought people were more likely to recognise my commitment to my job. I'd forfeit perceived indulgence, a massage, the gym, a blow-dry, because it was easier to be tough on myself, and I was in a scarcity mindset. I wanted it to be harder than it was, because hardness was value. I later discovered that despite being driven, and excited by and committed to my career, I had low self-esteem and therefore did not feel worthy of specific markers of success, such as a healthy body, a loyal boyfriend, a six-figure salary ... Many of us operate in this scarcity mindset, which is a one-way ticket to emotional burnout. A scarcity mindset means that we automatically obsess about what we don't have. We don't feel deserving or worthy, and our mindset is conditioned to think that there is a lack of resource available. This can lead to jealousy, feelings of low self-worth, hyperfixation and short-term coping mechanisms, including self-destructive habits such as overeating, cancelling social plans and infidelity.

ARE YOU ADDICTED TO BEING BUSY?

When we complete tasks, are complimented on how successful we are, or are acknowledged for a certain behaviour, dopamine is released, which provides us with a happy stimulus. Dopamine is a feel-good release, and therefore we want more of it. Craving this pleasure hormone increases the chances that we will repeat the behaviour, and thus the cycle begins. You can get hooked on this rewarding experience. While you might consider this to be an addiction to being busy, what you are actually addicted to is the feeling you get from completing, achieving or progressing in your projects, plans and goals. We often think about addiction in relation to drugs, smoking, alcohol or food, but addiction is about being compulsively or physiologically dependent on something habit-forming. Busyness is habit-forming. This is not about being less ambitious – quite the opposite. It is about revising the way you spend your time and where you place your focus, and ensuring that the energy you expend is proportional to what you are getting back in return, while making busy time productive.

Set Yourself Up to *Win*

Choose a discipline that you have natural ability in, and a sport you are built to play. I was never going to be a prize runner. I hated running at school; I wasn't built for it, and I feel that criticising runners in adulthood has become a central part of my personality. But just because I wasn't going to get a medal for running, that didn't mean I couldn't be a phenomenal sports competitor. In fact, I dominated tennis, hockey and a bunch of other sports. With the exception of the shame I felt when I had to do PE class in my pants as punishment for forgetting my kit (can you actually believe that was a thing?!), I have never felt any shame or guilt about not being a good runner. It's never been an issue for me. I was too busy focusing on the things I could do where I *could* win. It's highly likely, if you're a burned-out, ambitious woman, that you feel pressure to be great at everything. The narrative is reinforced everywhere that we must be better, stronger, faster – but strangely, never smarter. Here's the thing; if women have had to work harder, be better and deliver more, the net result of that is that we are more capable, able and determined than anyone else. Setting yourself up to win isn't about doing the hardest thing, or forcing yourself into a job or a dress size that makes you miserable. Setting yourself up to win is about making a realistic assessment of your natural abilities, and then leaning into those. In an abundant mindset, as we have seen, there is room for everyone. The very reason there is room for everyone is because we aren't all the same. It's the sum of our differences that brightens the picture.

Eight *and* Two

Many of us tie our self-worth to what we achieve, and have been convinced by positive reinforcement delivered through films, media, celebrity and books that the goal should be to be an 'Octopus Woman'. The main problem here is that you don't have eight arms, babe. You have two. So if you're juggling enough for someone with eight, you'll drop a few things. I work on an eight-to-two method – of every eight tasks that I deem important, only two can be urgent.

With this in mind, you might feel that if you aren't doing lots of things, you aren't being productive. There is a tension here. High-performing people do commit much time and energy to the things that are important to them. What many of them have learned is how to choose what those things are, and to avoid relying on a toxic cycle of self-generated busyness. You can, as they say, become a busy fool. In *Daring Greatly*, Brené Brown writes about numbing behaviours that we use as armour against vulnerability. And lest you think the term 'numbing behaviours' doesn't apply to you, because you're not hooked on cocaine or alcohol, she clarifies by saying:

> One of the most universal numbing strategies is what I call crazy-busy. I often say that when they start having 12-step meetings for busy-aholics, they'll need to rent out football stadiums. We are a culture of people who've bought into the idea that if we stay busy enough, the truth of our lives won't catch up with us.

Many of us use busyness as a distraction; if you are always overwhelmed with work, too busy to take on anything else, or unable to sit in stillness, it's a very convenient excuse to avoid dealing with things you'd prefer not to. If you are struggling to quit a busyness addiction, here are two important questions to ask yourself:

1. What is it inside you that is being fulfilled by being busy?
2. What are you avoiding by being busy?

Zooming out and finding slowness amongst chaos is a skill. To start learning this skill, try to create a goal that allows you to feel satisfaction without it being connected to being busy. For example, reading a book, having conversations that aren't about work, going for a walk.

There are a number of negative realities you may face if you are addicted to busyness:

- You confuse being busy with being successful.
- You are never present.
- Anxiety is a dominating force in your life.
- You are less productive.
- You are consumed by your phone or tablet.
- Your creativity is reduced.
- Your mood can be negatively affected.
- You say yes to everything but rarely enjoy anything.
- Busyness props up your self-image.
- You dabble rather than commit fully to something.
- You lack discipline.

Remember: there is a difference between having a full life and a busy one.

WHAT IS COGNITIVE REFRAMING AND HOW CAN IT HELP ME?

Cognitive reframing is a psychological technique that consists of identifying and then challenging and changing the way situations, experiences, events, ideas, and/or emotions are viewed.

Between us, what this means is that you have a considerable amount of choice with regards to how you view things that happen to, near, for, against or around you. On page 160, we talked about the two types of reactions: emotional and logical. This is closely linked to reframing.

Reframing is the ability to objectively review a situation and change the way in which you see it. The classic trope would be the idea of seeing a glass as half-full or half-empty. Your perception of that glass and the liquid within it gives an insight into how you approach situations more broadly. Early in my career, I was given the opportunity to pitch for an exciting and meaningful piece of business. I didn't win the pitch and I was naturally upset, allowing my brain to continue to gaslight me into thinking I was worthless, that all my clients would leave and that I was terrible at my job. I spoke to a mentor about it. He told me two things. The first was that I should sit briefly with the feeling that told me all my clients would leave. Was I catastrophising, or was it a helpful way of redirecting me to sharpen up a process, service or communication stream? If so, what action should I take to progress the situation? Should I call the client to ask for feedback, check in with my team, renegotiate the fee? The idea here was that the gut feeling, although sometimes just anxiety, could be reframed to become an opportunity to improve a service. The second thing he told me, relating specifically to the 'me not winning the client' thing, was that the situation in which I found myself was not me losing. Rather, it was me delaying the time when I would win. In the agency world, things run like snakes and ladders. Sometimes you win, and sometimes you don't. I have found it to be sage advice to consider losses as delayed winnings.

It is difficult to view situations with this kind of perspective when they are deeply personal or emotive. However, taking a step back and trying to think of other frames to fit the situation into can be of immeasurable help as you search for smarter ways to think about perceived challenges.

How to *Practise* Reframing

A 2020 study at Queen's University used brain-based markers of new thoughts to show that we have more than 6,000 thoughts every single day[3] – and depending on your outlook, this can mean a lot of negative thoughts each day. Here's how to reframe them:

- Identify the negative thought or thoughts.
- Write down the details of the situations that have contributed to this negative thought, then write specifically what thoughts or images went through your mind.
- Think about what *kind* of negative thoughts you are experiencing. Most negative thoughts fall into a few common categories. Try and determine if your thought is: unrealistic, overly critical, judgemental, blame-based, fault-based, pessimistic, catastrophic, emotion-based.
- Challenge your initial reaction by asking yourself: Is there substantial evidence for my thoughts? Is there evidence against my thoughts? Am I attempting to interpret the situation without all the evidence? What would a close friend of mine think about the situation?
- Be aware of whether you are falling into a thought trap. A thought trap is a cognitive distortion. We over-focus on repetitive negativity and can start to spiral.
- De-identify your thoughts. Negative thoughts are most powerful when they are unconscious, because this is when we identify with them. If we identify with a negative thought, then there is no way to create space or distance from it, which is what can pull us into a negative downward spiral. When thoughts remain unconscious, we believe they are 100 per cent

true, even if there is no fact or logic behind them. Until we wake up and consciously evaluate them, they will continue harming us without resistance. By becoming aware of our negative thoughts as they are happening, we de-identify from them. This creates a very powerful space where we are granted the chance to take more control over our mental wellbeing. When we are no longer unconsciously guided by our negative thoughts, we can master – or reframe the thought and have more control over our future thoughts and behaviour.

- Examine the cost or harm of the negative thought.
- Look for the fact-based, intelligent reframing opportunity in the situation.

WILL IT MAKE THE BOAT GO FASTER?

Will It Make the Boat Go Faster? is a motivational and autobiographical book that tells the story of an ordinary person in an ordinary team who achieved something pretty extraordinary. Ben Hunt-Davis, the co-author, won a gold medal at the Sydney Olympics in 2000 as part of the men's rowing eight.

The training for this feat came with a huge level of commitment. Those involved needed to make significant changes to their lifestyles in order to be in with a chance of achieving their goal. As such, they created a simple rule: will it make the boat go faster? This is a great way of understanding clearly and quickly whether the action you are taking is directly, positively impacting your goal. I have found this to be an incredibly decisive way to work out the value of what you are doing, and very useful in establishing a true performance culture. In terms of applying systems and processes, have a think about the questions below:

- What do you want to accomplish?
- How will you do that?
- What are the primary tasks you need to perform to make that happen?

THE BUSYNESS DETOX

In 2018, following a personal matter (boyfriend at the time got someone else pregnant while we were together), I became obsessed with the topic of lying. I read *Duped*, *Lying*, *Why We Lie*, and a series of other books. I found it fascinating that honesty is one of the most important, defended, protected and honoured values we all hold – and yet, it is entirely subjective. We lie to our children constantly, we lie to each other to protect the feelings of those we care about, and, crucially, we lie to ourselves. One of the biggest lies we tell relates to our productivity and what we deserve as a consequence of it. When we are overwhelmed by busyness, it can become impossible to see the wood for the trees, and although there are many great practices available in this book, it may be that you need a full factory reset. A Busyness Detox is a great way to check in with where you are at, and start the process of figuring your shit out.

A Busyness Detox is a conscious commitment to de-busying yourself, and building awareness around where your time could be better spent.

An ideal time frame for this practice is seven days, although five days will also work – and, frankly, at this point, a twenty-four-hour stint will do wonders. It's all workable. The crucial thing about this is that you set everything up on day one, so there's no extra lifting for you throughout the rest of the week.

- **Write down what you are trying to achieve through this process.** For example, perhaps you want to have more time for your partner, carve out stillness in your day, get home earlier or read more.
- **Start keeping notes.** Either using the Notes app on your phone or a notebook, make a note of every time you do something for the approval of others.
- **Create clarity for yourself with regards to what makes the boat go faster.** Stick to only doing those things. If you feel yourself participating in tasks that add zero value to this goal, make a quick note. This is useful for building accountability and reflecting on the week.
- **Drown out the noise.** Quieten, remove or minimise notifications on your phone, and other devices.

- **Keep your screen clean.** Delete apps you don't use regularly or those that tempt you into anything you would consider mindless.
- **Set yourself up to win.** Consider the kind of environment you need to be in to feel the emotion you desire. For me, the need to participate in a busyness detox always comes when I feel totally over-stimulated, and am seeking calm. As such, I cancel social plans, only listen to *Harry Potter* audiobooks or relaxing music, book a massage at the local parlour (where they are reassuringly cheap and reassuringly rude in equal measure), sign up for some gentle exercise classes, light a candle when I get home, plan my day, etc. You will have your own version of this.
- **When asked how you are, try not to reply with 'I'm busy.'**
- **Consider the behaviour you are trying to create.** You want to try and create alignment with that. For example, ask yourself 'What would a calm person do?' or 'What would an efficient person do?' This is helpful because it allows you to sense-check your behaviour in a conscious way, as you create new patterns and responses.
- **Don't tell everyone about it.** We all have a tendency to overshare, but this one is about retaining ownership for yourself. When you're doing a Busyness Detox, the goal is not to invite opinions. You don't want to

generate responses or more noise for yourself. By all means, share afterwards, but not during.

- **Switch to mono-tasking.**
- **Don't spend your evenings planning shit.** This was monumental for me. I spent many an evening planning holidays, dinners for friends, what I was going to do next week, what I wanted my gym routine to look like. What I was doing was just extending my work day. I was creating work and busyness for myself at a time that should have been more precious. I now try and take half an hour in the day to think about these things, rather than letting them ruin my evening and make my brain busy before bed.
- **Let's talk about baths.** Here's the thing: if you have a tub, go for your life. But don't confuse plunging into warm water with self-care. As above, you've got to figure out what the optimal environment is for you. It might be calling a friend for an hour, making your favourite meal, painting, listening to a podcast, watching *Real Housewives*, reading a book (hopefully this one), practising yoga, doing meditation, sewing or staring at the wall. There isn't a wrong or right way to do this. The point is that you need to find connection to the things that enhance your mindset – for you. And the things that work for you will likely be different to the things that work for other people. Having a bath, meditating and slathering yourself in

lavender butter might work for someone online, but it sure as shit won't ensure that I have an evening sans anxiety.

- **Be gentle.** In a Busyness Detox week, I usually work two days from home (one more than usual), move meetings where I can, start a little later (9.30am), and eat reasonably healthily. Remove the things from your week, where possible, that take away from your goal.
- **Think about what you have.** So much of what we see online encourages us to consider what we don't have. We can feel inferior, overweight, unloved, underpaid. Comparison really is the thief of joy, and that's what drives consumerism; making people think they are without, so they purchase more. Or, in this case, tricking ourselves into thinking we are doing more than we are in order to create something that resembles success. Newsflash: you have a huge amount of control over the way you apply yourself. In your detox week, try and consider all that you have, and read up on the abundance mindset.
- **Do something for someone else.** That might be buying a hot meal for a homeless person, or spending an evening a week volunteering. We all have different schedules, so find the best fit for you. You'll be amazed by how intentionally giving your time to someone who appreciates it, needs it and gives thanks for it, goes a long way towards giving you some perspective.

IT GETS EASIER

If you take only one thing away from this chapter, it should be this. Being burned out, miserable, tired all the time, unfulfilled and anxious is not how your life is intended to be. Our own experiences shape who we are, and many of us experience trauma beyond what we believe could be survivable. Our resilience, determination, courage and compassion allow us to continue putting one foot in front of the other. We have been led to believe that women are victims of this over-sensitised, overworked, under-appreciated echo chamber. We aren't. We have the power and resolve to create the life we want, and to be the architects of our own destiny. Pleasing others, being too busy to think, and creating value by never having a free moment, is not conducive to living a fulfilled life. There are smarter ways to work, and to live. As we get older, our knowledge and ability accumulates. We get better. And it gets easier. It is about mastery, not elimination.

CHAPTER 9

Move

'Exercise is the most potent and underrated antidepressant.'

BILL PHILLIPS

Movement and fitness changed my life, but at the beginning of my conscious smarter journey, I didn't understand the difference they could make. In this chapter, we will look at the different ways in which we can nourish ourselves through movement. I will ask you to create your own definitions of what is important to you, and I will describe how sleep is the elixir of life (and how to not get enraged when people tell you that sleep is the elixir of life). We will explore why being accountable for your own behaviour is the key to your success, and I will show you how a 'to-don't' list can help sharpen your focus, and how your environment shapes your outlook on life. This chapter has been written to spur you into action and help move you forward with your smarter goals.

FIND YOUR OWN DEFINITIONS

An important part of working smarter is to establish definitions that are owned by you. So often we hold ourselves to the standards of others, which ultimately means that we deny ourselves personal satisfaction. For example, your definition of fitness might be to compete in a triathlon. My definition of fitness might be jogging for ten minutes. If I judge myself against the definition you have set, I will forever be a failure. Another example relates to work–life balance. For me, a good work–life balance might be working in a job I love, fitting in the gym and having a nanny. For you, it might be a part-time role with flexible hours, and being at home with your children most of the time. Neither choice is better than the other, and it doesn't make sense to compare them. The first step towards achieving balance in your life is to understand what balance means to you. It's much easier to make decisions about what does and doesn't work for us when we have clear definitions. This is also the first step towards creating healthy boundaries.

Use the space below to write down your own definitions of these key areas:

Activity	Definition
Fitness	
Diet/food	
Healthy alcohol consumption	
Work satisfaction	
Success	
Happiness	
Balance	
Meaningful family time	
Self-development	

If you are dictating your success based on the definitions of others, consider whether you want to be defined by someone else.

If you are unhappy with the way things are, there are only ever two choices: change your mindset, or change your environment. Either you can change the way you view things, so that the current situation becomes acceptable to you, or you can change the way things are. I spent many years trying to change my mindset so that I could be happy with the weight I was. I was heavily influenced by social media and the growing feminist narrative that I ought to be happy with my body, including stretch marks and the parts of me that I didn't like. I was attempting to force acceptance of something that was ultimately counterintuitive for me, and this led me to unhealthy habits. The pressure that I felt turned into shame; was I anti-feminist for admitting that I wanted to lose weight, earn more money or 'have it all'? After a decade of mental and physical work, I realised that option two was the better path for me; I was going to change my situation. In losing weight, I created a healthier environment for myself, a happier relationship with myself and an abundant mindset, and set myself up for longer-term success. Losing weight became a by-product of finding healthier and happier ways to show up for myself, rather than using it as a marker of how successful or unsuccessful I was.

THE TO-DON'T LIST

The goal of smarter working is not endless to-do lists because, as we know, there are only three big decisions required on any given day. Smarter working is about identifying your workload, understanding the difference between urgent and important, delegating what you can, eliminating other tasks, allocating the amount of time you think a task will take, and matching those tasks to your energy, respecting your natural rhythms. In all the productivity books I have read (and there are many), the focus is always on to-do lists. I have found these useful in some respects, but on reflection, I have also found that they can add to stress. They are another metric by which I end up feeling that I am not performing. They are also, at their core, unproductive. I felt encouraged to make them as long as possible, adding endless tasks mindlessly, and feeling as though, if I didn't tick everything off, I wasn't working hard enough.

Instead, I have learned that in order to really commit to patterns of behaviour that I feel are valuable, I needed to focus on avoiding automatic habits as much as I did on creating new ones. As such, I consider a 'to-don't' list to be an important tool as I move through the day in a positive way.

A to-don't list is simply a list of tasks throughout the day (or week) that you want to avoid doing. Unlike a to-do list, which focuses on what you need to get done, a to-don't list helps you to identify the habits and behaviours that are holding you back.

In order to help you get started, here are some examples from my own to-don't list.

- Don't drink coffee after 2pm.
- Don't take my phone to the bathroom.
- Don't schedule meetings for a Friday afternoon.
- Don't react immediately if something annoys me.
- Don't skip Pilates.

I use the to-don't list in my professional life, but it's also helpful in my personal life. For example:

- Don't beat myself up if I don't finish reading a book.
- Don't immediately offer to pay on a date.
- Don't look at TikTok late at night on my phone in bed.
- Don't buy a litre bottle of Diet Coke, because I will drink the whole thing and feel terrible.
- Don't go to bed after midnight.
- Don't say yes to parties I know I won't want to attend.

There is something satisfying about reviewing your to-don't list and congratulating yourself on the self-control and willpower it has taken to stick to the list.

Making Your Own *To-Don't List*

To understand what your own list might look like, you can start by considering an action you have taken today and asking yourself three questions:

1. Was the activity worth it?

2. Did I enjoy it?
3. Did it add value to my day?

Think about the habits and behaviours that are holding you back from being productive or are impacting your health. These could be anything from spending too much time on social media to leaving work tasks to the last minute. Much of the time, boredom compels us to let our minds wander as we seek out stimulation. Knowing and understanding your own unhealthy patterns and using that awareness to limit them can help with longer-term success, leading you to a smarter way of working.

If you are struggling to create your to-don't list, begin by imagining your worst possible work day. This can help you to identify the behaviours and actions you'd like to eliminate.

Tips for Making Your *To-Don't List*

- Take a few minutes to write down the habits you want to avoid during the day, then choose your top three to focus on first. Not all habits are created equal, and giving yourself too much to 'not' do can be demoralising. Prioritise your list based on the habits that are having the biggest negative impact on your life.

- At the end of the day, tick them off if you didn't do them.
- If there's something on there you didn't manage to stick to, try setting a more achievable way of avoiding it for tomorrow. For example, if today's to-don't was 'Don't check social media during working hours', then tomorrow try 'Don't check social media between 9am and 12pm.'
- Try this for two weeks and adjust your list each day to make sure you're ticking off each to-don't. By the end of the two weeks, you should be able to focus on the things you want to do, rather than being held back by the things you don't.

This simple yet powerful tool can help you stay focused, increase productivity and increase balance. By identifying the habits and behaviours that are holding you back and consciously avoiding them, you can create a more productive and smarter daily routine.

EXERCISE

Moving your body makes your brain happier. Well, in theory it does. Chemically, it does. But much of this depends on your approach to it. I'll let you in on a secret and save you some time.

The only exercise that you should be doing is exercise that either makes you stronger or makes you happier, or ideally a combination of the two.

In the past, I would watch as my boyfriend practically skipped out of the gym with a semi after a workout, while I felt drained and quite down. I was hanging out for the huge burst of energy I had been told to expect, but it never came. I thought I must not be working hard enough. My relationship with exercise, for more than a decade, was purely punitive. The success of the workout depended on how difficult it was, how sore I felt, and how hungry I could make myself. I did double Barry's classes, boxing, every gym class going, back-to-back spinning and weights sessions with a personal trainer. I was miserable. My approach to exercise was not smart. I was always exhausted, I didn't feel strong or fit or healthy, and it dominated my thoughts. I set unrealistic expectations, obviously didn't meet them, and then reminded myself I was a failure. I never hit my fitness or weight-loss goals, and I felt a paralysing sense of hopelessness.

Double It

About five years ago, I changed my outlook by reframing my approach to exercise, and it altered my health journey forever. I lost just over 40kg, although the weight loss became secondary to the other benefits. The first thing I did was take the time frame in which I had set my goals, and double it. Sounds simple, right? The grace I gave myself in taking the time that was required to undo decades of learned behaviour, ingrained habits and repetitive self-loathing was like taking a deep breath. The self-imposed time frames I had previously landed on were incompatible with my busy life, and required more commitment that I was able to give. I was thrashing my body in extreme and short-term bursts, which led me to – you guessed it – burn-out. In addition, I hated exercise. I resented it, feared it, felt frustrated by it. I felt I should have been fitter than I was. I remember googling whether exercise simply didn't work for some people . . .

If one process worked for everyone, the diet and exercise industry would be a lot smaller and a lot quieter. The lesson here is that the smartest way to exercise is to find the right way for *you*. For me, an active lifestyle is preferable – cycling to work (if the weather is good), walking in nature, hiking in the summer, renting a kayak on the coast in the UK in the summer. Being outside and active changes my brain positively. I learned that I didn't have to ruin myself in the gym to find endorphins, or to change my physical appearance. I learned that while hardcore exercise can improve fitness and muscle density, for me the cross-trainer and reformer Pilates are my go-to methods of finding peace and balance, plus the additional benefits that I want. You might have to shop around to find the right combo for you, but it's definitely not the hardest workout available. As someone who weighed over 100kg, I know it is difficult for people who have never been overweight to understand the challenges that exist for bigger bodies: how much harder it all is, and how you might have to modify exercises to make them achievable. How it feels to skip the gym if you don't have something to tie around your waist, as your cellulite shows through your gym leggings. Why you can't have a shower after the class, because the towels supplied are the size of a postage stamp. The fear of a beach holiday. The pressure to pack everything you could possibly need for a weekend away, because if you forget something, you can't just borrow it from your friends. I do regret how many things I said no to, how many things I missed out on, and how much I denied myself. My hope is that you are able to find the strength and courage to change your situation if it no longer serves you.

Remember:

- Movement should be enjoyable
- Reframe the idea of exercise as punishment, and consider it to be kindness
- Take your gut health seriously
- Do the work to learn about what your body needs
- Consider exercise and movement and nourishment
- Double the time frame you set yourself

SLEEP

I remember everything about the day I stepped into the gym for my first personal-training session, largely because of my crippling anxiety, fear of failure, and thoughts that everyone would be looking at me and laughing at me. I also remember what my personal trainer said: 'You will never reach any of your fitness goals if you cannot unlock the power of sleep.' I rolled my eyes. Here we go, I thought. Chicken and broccoli and twelve hours of sleep a night. Sure. Although the presentation of the information made me take him less seriously, the essence of the suggestion lingered. It was almost as though it was too simple, and the coping mechanism I had created for not fulfilling my true potential was to overcomplicate things. Simplicity scared me, because it offered nowhere to hide.

What I know now is that sleep is integral to my mental and physical health, and my ability to achieve in the way I want to. Things fall into place more easily when I am well rested. My skin is better. I make better choices. I have more patience. I dress better. I feel healthier. I am more generous with myself and others. I think I retain less water, but this is not a white paper, so calm down. These are some of the personal benefits I notice when I sleep well.

I'd like to caveat all of this with a small note that says that I do believe that success is directly proportionate to the sacrifices you're willing to make, that there are times where getting less sleep is a reality, and that we aren't aiming for perfection here. We are aiming for a commitment to a more nurturing, smarter way of arming yourself for a world in which you can achieve anything.

Two things had to happen for me to evolve my relationship with sleep.

Firstly, I had to change my mindset. Throughout my career, in fact, throughout my entire life, I had been fed subtle variations of toxic sleep-deprivation tactics being paramount to success. Being able to achieve more on fewer hours of sleep was a status symbol. At school, at university, and in my working life, the idea of productivity being imminently more impressive on a sleep deficit was a sign of someone being a high achiever. I thought that getting up early (I was told 5am was the sweet spot), not wearing make-up (because I was too busy and not vain), being the first one in and the last one out, sleeping in the office and having a caffeine addiction meant that I was a great businesswoman. I can categorically share with you that this is not the case. I had to really challenge myself to consider an alternative perspective. In my old mindset, I had taken masculine, toxic, outdated, unsustainable and unhealthy attitudes towards sleep and productivity and viewed them as markers for success.

If you look hard enough for something, you'll find it. The social media I consumed was of people doing THE MOST. Forget sleep, they were sharing routines where they woke up to a 5am alarm of applause before reading an entire book, birthing a child, cleaning the house, doing the weekly shop, having a blow-dry, and weight training for two hours before arriving in the office in a Stella McCartney suit for a 9am meeting. I wanted to be like them! What I now know is that these videos are a huge distortion of reality. They don't show the nannies, the home gym, the life of their partner, whether their company was profitable, how the person feels throughout the day, the way they treat others, or the reality of the output of their seemingly incredibly productive routines. These videos don't consider the unpaid work that takes up our time, our emotional bandwidth, our feelings of desperation for acceptance or our fear of failure. They don't show the many holidays or the weekends. They only showed me part of the picture – and it was a part that made me feel like a worthless piece of shit.

This was combined with a total sense of revulsion when faced with the available advice surrounding sleep. Actually go fuck yourself if you tell me to buy a light that wakes me up like the sun would. Have I tried meditation? Yes, of course I have, but it didn't work because I can't create stillness in my overactive mind as I consider all the ways in which I failed today. Once, in a moment of weakness and boredom, I tried *all* the things. No phone before bed, installing a dimmer switch, taking a bath, reading a book, performing an elaborate ceremony where I seduced myself with a candle and some pillow spray, while panicking about what would happen if I fell asleep with a naked flame still lit . . . Obviously none of it worked, because sleep wasn't a priority for me. It also made me cross, because the ceremony of it all felt like a completely unrealistic nightly ritual. As someone who doesn't wear mascara because it's too time-consuming to remove, it felt obscene to waste all this time on such luxuries.

I needed to focus on prioritising sleep in a way that worked for me. My sleep routine now isn't terribly elaborate. I don't speak to my friends or family on the phone after 7pm, generally, because I find it too stimulating. I try to avoid films, reality television and social media after 8pm because a) I save them for the gym to habit pair (see page 144), and b) I tend to absorb the drama I am watching. I don't read enough, but I do listen to *Harry Potter* audiobooks or sounds of thunder. I don't lay out all my clothes or pack my lunch every day (I do it most days).

I do, however, fiercely protect my sleep, and feel no shame about waking up at 8am, napping on a Saturday afternoon if I am tired, or excusing myself from an event early because I'd prefer to be in bed. I don't have expensive bed sheets or an expensive bed, nor do I invite a shaman to bless the mattress before I crawl in. I simply make sleep a priority, considering it the most important time for my mind and body to rest, recover and reset.

I understand that there are exceptions where you might have to deviate from your sleep plan, but good boundary-setting should help you return to the right pattern for you. My sleep routine is the right one for me, and yours might be different. I know eating sugar before bed makes me hyper, that if I've had a work event, it might take me more time to wind down, and that if I am physically and mentally exhausted, arriving at the office a little later than usual the next day will probably be fine. Sleep is a superpower, and it unlocks your potential across everything else that you do. Prioritise it, commit to it, and fall into a routine that works for you.

ACCOUNTABILITY

If you want to hide from the work, you might as well hide from the money too.

Accountability is an essential trait of an ambitious person looking to live and work smarter. Being accountable for the environment in which you exist can unlock a new era of thriving.

When you're personally accountable, you take ownership of what happens as a result of your choices and actions. You don't blame others or make excuses, and you do what you can to make amends when things go wrong.

To become more accountable, make sure that you're clear about your roles and responsibilities.

As writer and researcher Maggie Wooll explains: 'Accountability is closely related to self-discipline, because it demands that you remain honest about your actions and intentions.'[1]

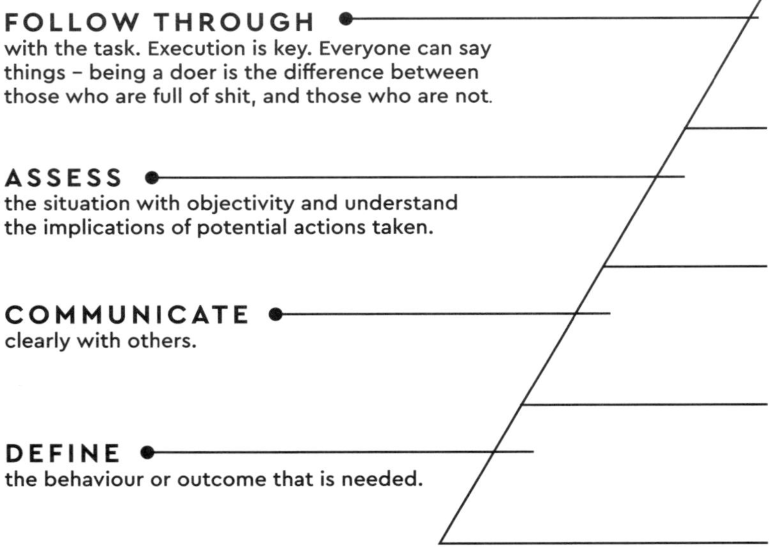

ESTABLISHING ACCOUNTABILITY COMES DOWN TO THESE FOUR STEPS:
FOLLOW THROUGH
with the task. Execution is key. Everyone can say things – being a doer is the difference between those who are full of shit, and those who are not.
ASSESS
the situation with objectivity and understand the implications of potential actions taken.
COMMUNICATE
clearly with others.
DEFINE
the behaviour or outcome that is needed.

How to Create More *Accountability*

- Learn your likes and dislikes.
- Discover your beliefs and values.
- Know your personal boundaries.
- Identify and accept your personality traits.
- Understand your role in a team.
- Identify a clearer path in your professional life.
- Understand how you interact with others.
- Recognise your core personal values.
- Increase your capacity for self-compassion.
- Have a clearer idea of, and become more connected to, your life's purpose.
- Know what it takes to be self-motivated.
- Be more adaptable.

SMART GOALS

SMART goals are a commitment to criteria that can help keep you moving to complete a task. You can tag in SMART goals if you feel that you aren't able to close the loop on projects that feel important to move you closer to the desired outcome. Our focus can shift over time, and unforeseen factors can change the course of what would have otherwise been a perfect plan.

Creating clear criteria is essential here. Goal-setting can be a lofty, imaginative process. Many people fail to achieve their goals because they haven't put in place specific criteria or systems and processes to help them get there. The setting of the goal is not enough. Our environment evolves, changes and moves, which can make it difficult to keep moving towards our goals if we don't have clear parameters in place by which those goals are defined. Setting SMART goals will help you to feel more connected to the origins of your vision, and more likely to continue to be focused, even when the world is moving around you.

Set goals that are SMART:

- Specific – make your goal super specific, or else you'll wander in the vagueness.
- Measurable – set some measures, otherwise you won't be able to assess progress.
- Achievable – ensure that you can actually complete the task in the time allocated. Set yourself up to win.
- Relevant – mostly, the goals you are working towards should align with your value system, and encourage emotional investment.
- Time-bound – set an end date and schedule check-ins within the time frame to make sure that you stay accountable.

This provides clear direction and makes tasks more manageable. It also allows you to create positive reinforcement of the types of behaviour that you want to inhabit on a long-term basis.

The *Prediction* Machine

Our brains are prediction machines. What this means in practice is that when we view a particular scenario, our brains do not require intricate detail to make up our minds about how we feel. As such, we have to fight hard to break those predictive patterns. Using SMART goals will help you stay connected to the longer-term vision, even if the daily distractions lead you off course.

Assistant professor of psychiatry at the University of Toronto, Dr Ralph Lewis, writes that 'Consciousness enhances the brain's ability to form predictive models of the environment and the self. Faulty top-down influence of expectation on perception shapes illusions, weird beliefs, anxiety, depression, psychosomatics and more.'[2] He also refers to the work of Anil Seth, a neuroscientist and author of *Being You: A New Science of Consciousness*, who 'suggests that even our perceptions of what is presently out there are, in a sense, just predictions or simulations (what he refers to as "controlled hallucinations"). These are formed by a continual process of updating predictions or assumptions ("best guesses") as to what the sensory data are perceiving.'

What the eff does all this mean? People see what they want to see. Perception and reality for all of us can be distorted as a consequence of our experiences, both positive and negative. Our 'outlook' on life is shaped personally, and sometimes it can be difficult to understand, or imagine, why someone else's opinion on something differs to what we believe to be true.

Remember the viral 'Is it blue, is it gold?' dress? It caused such a sensation because those who identified it as blue were vehement in their vision, and those who saw it as gold felt the same. The most common image that demonstrates alternate perception is this:

Originally published in 1892, this German cartoon divides viewers with an optical illusion that asks you to see either a duck or a rabbit. If you see a duck, and it's then explained to you that it can also be a rabbit, the image becomes clearer. Without the explanation or alternate perception, you might be steadfast in identifying it as a duck. Anil Seth, in his famous TED Talk, says:

> Perception – figuring out what's there – has to be a process of informed guesswork in which the brain combines these sensory signals with its prior expectations or beliefs about the

> way the world is to form its best guess of what caused those signals. The brain doesn't hear sound or see light. What we perceive is its best guess of what's out there in the world.[3]

Smart people understand perception and accountability as important factors in decision-making. It is very easy to blame others for the decisions we make, or to assume that things happen to us. They don't. If there are five reckless and irresponsible people in a room, then you are the sixth. If you only look at slim, attractive people online, and feel worse about your own self-image, you need to be accountable for the content to which you are exposing yourself. If you are suffering from anxiety on a Monday morning, but made your body into a chemistry set over the weekend, did no exercise and ate ultra-processed food, the problem is not your job. I spent a long time apportioning blame to others for situations for which I was entirely responsible. I had a slower metabolism, I found it harder to retain information, I was big-boned (remember that one . . . ?). The point at which I began the process of becoming more accountable, more aware of myself, and more able to consider situations with objectivity, rather than falling into habits, was also the point at which I began to change my life. In a room of five high-achieving go-getters, you're the sixth. Be the sixth. This will enable you to objectively consider the environment you are creating for yourself, and the ability you have to change it.

MOVING ON FROM BAD HABITS

Moving on is one of the most difficult things to do, whether it's from a traumatic job ending, a relationship that hurt you, a friendship where it all went wrong, a fight where they really said some shit, a great loss, grief, self-loathing – all the bad stuff. We carry it through life, accumulating mental, physical and emotional weight, until it can all feel really heavy. At the start of my health journey, I met with a hypnotist whom I went to see for binge-eating disorder. The first thing he said to me was, 'I am not a nutritionist, and you do not have a problem with food.' Overeating was my *solution*; the problem was something entirely different. Diets wouldn't work for me, because they weren't addressing the cause. In my career, I didn't ask for the money I deserved for my skills, for no other reason than that I didn't believe I was worth it. I didn't write this book for ten years because I didn't think I was confidently able to share my learnings. When I began to take the steps required to move on from habits that no longer served me, I felt I was betraying my younger self. How could I look her in the eye when I'd defied all she stood for and lost weight, dressed well and been successful? It was very confusing.

As we move away from our broken selves, the universe throws us tests. Have you ever started a great new relationship, and then received a text from someone you hoped to never hear from again? Or accepted a job, and then been contacted by an old boss with a new opportunity? These are not coincidences.

They are tests. Tests to see whether you are really ready to move on and embrace what is waiting for you in the new life that you are choosing to create.

Tips for *Moving On* from Bad Habits

- Identify the habits you want to change. These might be brought to your awareness through the time-tracking exercise (see page 83).
- Acknowledge them.
- Write them on your to-don't list (see page 211).
- Consider the behaviour that you'd prefer to be displaying, and the opportunities you would like to embrace.
- Add these chosen behaviours to your Daily Dos.
- Check in on your environment, and ensure you are surrounding yourself with cues that help you towards the positive habits you have chosen.
- Think about what boundaries you might need to enforce to avoid slipping back into the bad habits you want to avoid.
- Remove as many triggers as possible.
- Use 'but'. Part of the stress of trying to break bad habits is the immediate self-shame we can suffer as we judge ourselves for not acting better. If you find

yourself slipping up (which will happen), try adding a but. For example:

- *'I'm overweight and can't wear the clothes I want,* **but** *I could be in shape a few months from now.'*
- *'I didn't get the job and I feel like an idiot,* **but** *I learned a lot from the interview process, which will help me next time.'*
- *'I feel like a failure,* **but** *everybody fails sometimes.'*

If you are still struggling to move on from a bad habit, you can bring some accountability to your behaviour by asking the questions below to improve your awareness:

- Is there a particular place where the habitual behaviour tends to happen?
- Is there a particular time of day when it tends to happen?
- How do you feel when it happens?
- Are other people involved?
- Does it happen right after something else?
- Are there any other triggers you can identify?

Replacing *Bad Habits*

So much of what we are taught in personal development is about habit-forming. Adopting new, good habits is the only way to reach your solution or goal, so it's a brilliant focus, but there is also much to be said for moving on from habits that don't serve you. Breaking 'bad' habits takes a high level of accountability and awareness. One way to move on from bad habits is to refocus your attention on corresponding good habits that can replace them. Try writing down some of the habits that you believe are keeping you from achieving your goals, and consider good habits you could adopt in their place.

Bad habit	**Good habit**
Answering questions that don't exist.	Accepting that not everything is that deep.
Guessing what other people think.	Asking people what they think.
Automatically complaining.	Seeking positives in challenging situations.
Criticising others.	Thinking about what that criticism really shows about how I feel.

Here's your own version to fill out:

Bad habit	Good habit

CHAPTER 10

Momentum

'Even if you are on the right track, you'll get run over if you just sit there.'

WILL ROGERS

Creating momentum in your personal and professional life feels great. It's easier to move through tasks, things just seem to go right, all the traffic lights turn green, good things seem to be happening for you, and ultimately, progress is made. While it is important to define what momentum feels like for you personally – in relationships, in the office, in your creative outlet – there are some basic principles of momentum that we all share. In this chapter, you'll learn how to create momentum when it feels like all the traffic lights are red – and why the goal is not to never fail. We'll look at how to achieve a flow state, why pointing in the right direction is the most efficient way to start a journey, and why discipline in ending your thoughts will open up a more seamless route to momentum for you.

TASK TENSION

As we now know, multitasking is a bust. Although there are certain tasks that can be done in parallel with one another, the big brain-drain ones need singular focus. Switching between tasks generates friction in all of them, and slows down momentum across everything that you do. One of the most important lessons in productivity is that tasks have to be completed in order to generate momentum. The circle has to roll.

IF THE CIRCLE ISN'T WHOLE, IT CANNOT ROLL

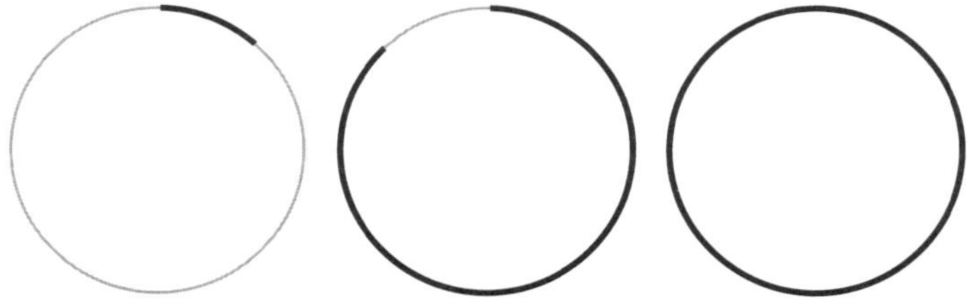

It doesn't matter whether it's ten per cent complete or ninety per cent complete, until the circle is whole, it cannot roll. In order to generate progress, to feel good and to reject limiting beliefs, you should view momentum as horse power, propelling you forwards, inspiring others around you, and creating value in what you are doing.

It's hard to spell and harder to pronounce, but at some point in your life you may have felt the Zeigarnik Effect: the tendency to think about uncompleted tasks more than completed tasks.[1] Researchers call this 'task tension' – the nagging feeling that helps you stay the course until you've achieved your goal. It's the basic psychology behind a brand teasing a campaign, a cliff-hanger at the end of your favourite Netflix show or the reason ticking something off your to-do list can feel so satisfying.

This is the chapter for you if you're someone who wants to know the ending of a film before you've watched it, or someone who reads the last page of a book, first. Task tension should be proportional to the urgency of the task. As we've already discussed, working out the difference between urgent and important, and sticking with three big decisions per day can help allocate your energy to what needs doing first. If you're in a place with your work where everything feels fucking urgent, you'll feel like all the tasks require all your energy all the time. When you're stuck in this death spiral, task tension will be high. You'll end up flitting between tasks, spending disproportionate amounts of time on them, overthinking, becoming anxious, rushing, self-doubting and self-sabotaging – not to mention occupying precious mental real estate thinking about this heady cocktail. This is the opposite of momentum or flow.

If you'd like a more visual analogy, consider the ultimate state of momentum or flow as building the wave, and then riding it.

Imagine watching a pro surfer gliding over the crest of a perfect wave, almost in slow motion. That's momentum. Now consider where you are. For me, I was swimming against the tide, someone had called the coastguard as I flailed around in the sea, and when I was pulled out by a nice man with a failed personal-training career, my bikini bottoms were round my ankles and the people on the beach were laughing. That, my friends, is not momentum.

Tip: One task at a time, with one achievable goal, will generate sustained focus and the momentum that comes with it. Multiple parallel tasks will scatter this. (See 'Mono-tasking', page 141.)

The *Task*, The *Ask*, The *Action*

This is a method that I have used effectively in my life when creating momentum and reducing task tension. Each project that you work on has three kick-off components:

- **The task:** What is the task at hand?
- **The ask:** What is it that I am being asked to do?
- **The action:** What do I need to do to make it happen, and how long will it take?

I hate to break it to you, but lots of people have good ideas. I've heard lots of them. I've had some pretty good ones myself. When Uber launched, I frequently heard people saying they had previously had the same idea. In an art gallery next to a blank canvas, whispers of, 'I could have done that myself' betray the cynic in the room. The point is very much being missed by these comments. The point is not whether you were *able* to do something. It's whether or not you *did* it. Execution is everything. Momentum is everything.

THE CHAMPAGNE GLASS

There are lots of analogies about task-juggling; people talk about spinning plates, simmering pans, balls in the air. None of them really work for me. I like to think about bubbles. It would be a shame for those bubbles to not be in a champagne glass.

Stick with me here. Imagine that each bubble is a task. They float upwards, in a straight line, determined to reach the surface as quickly and directly as possible. The reason that they rise in straight columns is due to the chemical compounds that give the drink flavour. Each bubble in the liquid creates a wake behind it as it rises, and other bubbles can get knocked around, or pushed off course, by this wake. If the glass is left for too long, the bubbles evaporate and the drink goes flat. If there are too many bubbles, the liquid erupts in an eager climax, spilling from the glass. The size of the bubble increases as it nears the surface, because the pressure decreases and the volume increases. Tasks often feel as though they grow in size right before they are finished.

The Smarter Method is not telling you to have fewer bubbles; I encourage you to have *all* the bubbles, and to remember that they are singular and identifiable in their individual form. They are also abundant and ever flowing, no matter how full the glass is. Consider the champagne flute the arena for your ideas, with the bubbles jostling, vibrating and seeking the surface. Each one needs to be completed in its entirety and maintain its own direct course. Crucially, a bubble is nothing without an edge around it. Preserving each task's own identity, making it a bubble, pointing it in the right direction and letting it go, will remind you that this isn't an exercise in doing less. Rather, it's a commitment to finding streamlined ways to do as much as you like. Sometimes, we can feel as though opportunities are going to pass us by. Our eagerness is not rooted in negativity – we find ourselves so excited and energised by the possibilities that we want to grab them all. For the overachiever, it feels as though burnout is a certainty. Approaching life with an abundant mindset allows you to relax into the reality that there is enough for everyone, and there is enough for you. Opportunities will not pass you by, because you are precisely where you need to be. The systems and processes that you are learning in this book will enable you to streamline all your bubbles.

Direction is *More Important* than Speed

When you're faced with hard things, you're told to put one foot in front of the other. You're told that if you're in hell, you should keep going. And you're challenged as to whether each move you make will make the boat go faster. All of these ideas rely on one crucial assumption: that you're facing in the right direction. Much of the literature on productivity and business encourages us to move fast, break things, sprint and time-travel, in order to reach our goals in the most streamlined way possible. The problem with this is that you might be going as fast as you can, but if you're zig-zagging, your time will be taken up with the three-point turns and dead ends that you're driving into at sixty miles an hour. These detours often make up the journey, but if the goal is getting from A to Z (crucially not A–B; what the fuck happens after B?), then step one is pointing yourself in the right direction. Step two is setting your course, ideally the most direct one. Step three is setting your speed, which will vary. Some days you will be able to sprint; other days you'll sit and have a rest. One day, you might hop on a Lime Bike or call an Uber and zip along, and on other days you might have heavy bags to carry. The speed is irrelevant. The most important part of any journey is to first establish whether or not you are going in the right direction. Many of us can find this to be a challenging point to reach, particularly on the eve of big birthdays, break-ups, changes at work, or after reading an article that tells us we are all probably barren and need to spend all our money freezing our eggs at twenty-eight years old to continue the development of humanity. Self-doubt can paralyse us into not knowing which way is up, and burnout is a painful state of fear, perceived lack of control, anxiety, fatigue and apathy.

How to Point Yourself in the *Right Direction*

- First, be clear on your destination. You can't start a drive without a destination in mind.
- Be real and honest with yourself: if the current direction doesn't feel right, acknowledge that and work out why.
- Set your course. Having a plan is important.
- Double the timeline. Don't set yourself up to fail with unrealistic deadlines.
- Conduct an MOT. Before a long journey, cars are usually checked for fuel, windscreen wash, tyre pressure, a spare tyre – and of course, you'll need snacks. So before you set out, consider whether you have everything you need. Do you need a Busyness Detox (see page 202) or some help from an expert in order to get ready for the drive?
- Connect with the question: 'Will it make the boat go faster?' If you are aware of where you are going, why and how, it's much easier to invite people, places, thoughts and things into your life that fit in with that journey, rather than being distracted by detours.
- Make it more enjoyable. Invite a friend, create a playlist, enjoy the ride.

- Pay attention to your fuel gauge and look out for punctures. In other words, know and understand when you are approaching burnout. Being able to identify signs of burnout in your behaviour is one of the most important tools of self-connection and self-awareness. Think of this as deciding which way to turn at a junction. Old me would have turned left, sped past several warning signs, ignored the terrain change to a mountainous ravine, and continued on with half a tank, broken AC, a flat tyre and coyotes circling. Smarter me would turn right, on to a newly tarmacked motorway, listening to *The Rest is History* so I can, at some point (when?), competently discuss the fall of the Roman Empire, with a huge bag of three-for-two M&S snacks, and a jerry can in the back in case of emergency. The steering wheel turns both ways. You have a choice about which route you take.

SUCCEED MORE TIMES THAN YOU FAIL

'Don't worry about failure; you only have to be right once.'

Drew Houston, founder and CEO of Dropbox

Failure is not to be avoided at all costs. In fact, the moment at which I was able to fully embrace, consider and become comfortable with the idea that I might fail, it became a far less scary outcome. Although I don't think about failing all the time, and nor do I ultimately want to fail, my understanding that it is a possibility means that it sits smaller in my perfect picture. It also means that I have become comfortable with the fact that if I do fail, I will likely be fine. I'd adjust, I'd figure it out. It's less of a threat to my survival, as it's no longer a big, scary, undesirable outcome. For many of us, especially women, we have been led to believe that we must exist in a faultless, perfect world. The idea of a misstep, lateral movement or singular failures ties us up in layers of shame, humiliation and regret. But, as we now know, perfection isn't the goal. Using the Smarter Method, we reconsider and reframe the way we see failure. The goal is not to omit it. The goal is to succeed more times than you fail. The goal is to make the circle roll.

TAKE WHAT YOU NEED

For almost the first decade of my career, I was obsessed with the idea of having mentors. I hadn't yet learned to have my own definitions, so I adopted those of others. As such, I was searching for a group of highly competent people to cheerlead for me, meet me once a month for lunch and tell me how I could be better in my work life. Back when I started my company in the Stone Age, the idea of a mentor was something quite formal, generally a relationship that took place at a table in a central London restaurant on a Tuesday lunchtime. I found a group of such people, and hung off every word they said. I made decisions about my work and life based on their opinions and I formed incredibly disrupted patterns of momentum by changing direction following my meetings with them.

What I now know is that not all advice is good advice. You do not have to adopt the opinions of others when they share advice with you, and you can be comfortable outgrowing people, places and things that once served you as oracles. I am no longer working with any of the people who mentored me when I was in my twenties, and I consider that to be a positive thing. We give so much power to the opinions of others, and it can be completely derailing to our own journey, breeding self-doubt, an uncomfortable pace and a connection to what is seen rather than felt. It is really important to let go of the opinions, advice and information that don't serve you, and to curate the opinions that really matter to you.

The same approach is true for social media. I have interviewed over 100 successful entrepreneurs for my podcast, and I ask all of them whether they have a good relationship with social media. More than half only focus on the account for their own business, and almost all say that they limit how much they look at the accounts of their competitors. It wouldn't be terribly efficient to listen to 100 hours of podcasting to learn this lesson, so in the spirit of this book, I shall summarise. Almost all of these entrepreneurs find it to be less inspiring, less abundant and less positive to pick over what their competitors seem to be doing. They have identified, and therefore commit to, a form of censorship that focuses them on what they are doing, rather than absorbing the work of others around them.

The idea of a mentor has evolved in recent years. Your mentor could be an Instagram account, a book, a podcast, a successful entrepreneur whom you've never met, an old boss or a new friend. The important thing is to surround yourself with those who share abundantly. Do this, and you might find you've got mentors all around, in different forms. You can take and leave information as you see fit – it's not all right for you, and it's important to know that there are reasons why you consider some opinions more powerful than others.

CATASTROPHISING

Have you ever had the faintest whiff of a stressful thought that very quickly grows into the most horrific scene on all of God's green earth? Same. It's a cool trick my brain plays on me that paralyses me and makes me completely unable to deal with the actual challenge at hand. It burns emotional and physical energy as I play out all the imaginary scenarios and how I might feel about them if and when they happened.

When you catastrophise, your brain is creating a reality for you as a consequence of your thoughts, and this can trigger a fight-or-flight response, even if you aren't actually encountering the thing you are catastrophising about. This is a lesson I learned as I steered what felt like a sinking ship through the Covid-19 pandemic. I found myself speaking in extremes and conflating issues. If a client handed in their notice, I would parrot to my friend on the phone that evening that 'all of my clients were leaving'. If a guy didn't text me back, I'd think, 'I'm a disgusting pig who doesn't deserve love.' If I didn't win the pitch, it would be, 'I might need to pivot my whole business, as I'm obviously not good enough.'

Speaking in extremes is something many of us automatically do to manage our own expectations. We entertain the most extreme version of a situation in order to prepare ourselves for the worst-case scenario. The problem with this habit is that you are using energy on imaginary scenarios that don't exist, rather than addressing the specific issue at hand. As we know with momentum, each circle has to roll. It's important not to conflate issues; instead, we need to deal with one thing at a time, separately.

If you continue blowing air into the balloon, at some point, it will pop. You don't need to empty all the air in your lungs each time something problematic happens. You must think about the task, the ask and the action, then finish the thought and let the circle roll.

Finishing the Thought

This is a real skill that will enhance your life. I spent much of my twenties catastrophising and looping negative thoughts constantly, overplaying them with outrageous fancy outcomes, living the anxiety over and over again. I felt as though I had very little control over my emotions and was often exhausted by the constant circularity of these negative imaginings or 'running thoughts'. Later, I discovered that this was connected to my obsessive compulsive disorder (OCD), but even if you do not have a diagnosis of OCD, it's quite common to find it difficult to end thoughts. The long-term issue with this is that you are burning significant mental energy on imaginary scenarios and triggering a constant state of high alert. Just as finishing a task enables you to close the circle and let things roll forward, being able to end the thought and close the loop is a skill that enhances both productivity and momentum.

There are two clear options available to you if you are experiencing running thoughts. The first is to change your thought patterns. The second is to change how you *feel* about these thoughts.

Changing or Disrupting Thought Patterns

This is where most of the advice I received led me: a confrontation of negative thoughts and the suggestion of a total overhaul of my entire thought process and emotional make-up. No small feat. I struggled with the idea that I could change how I felt, because, well, that was how I felt. It's still not my preferred route, although with hypnotherapy and cognitive behavioural therapy (CBT), it is possible to change your end-to-end thought pattern.

Changing *How You Feel* About Running Thoughts[2]

The shift that I made, which I have found to be very rewarding, is that I changed my perception of running thoughts. Rather than trying to eliminate them completely, I accepted them as part of my mental make-up, and sought to alter my former demonic tether to them. If I could change my relationship to my thoughts rather than trying to change their content, I would be able to unlock a superpower. Although technically a form of momentum, negative running thoughts probably aren't the wind you'd like behind your sails. They can become incredibly dominant and distracting to your goals. In addition, we often dwell on and consider negative variations more than positive ones. This isn't a bad thing; we want a strong connection to our gut, and assessing risks and analysing outcomes is a crucial part of our evolution. The problem is not having these thoughts in the first place, it's that we have demonised and held on to them.

I would like to share some helpful ways to end the thought and stop it from running away with you, but in order to do so, I must reluctantly promote a version of journaling. My main issue with journaling is that I think it has been romanticised, leading us to focus more on the pen, the light splintering through the window, and the way we will deliver the news in our morning meetings that we journaled that morning. I'd like to simplify things by just encouraging you to write the thoughts down, in whatever form works for you at the time, in whatever maniacal structure they come out. Read them, then delete or discard them. This is a helpful exercise for two reasons. The first, because it allows you to remove the thoughts from inside your head. The second, because in deleting them/throwing them away, you are taking the physical action of discarding them in order to remind yourself that they are transient.

Here are some more tips for ending thoughts:

- **Stop arguing with yourself.** Cinematically, in marketing campaigns and television adverts, we've been encouraged to consider decision-making as battling with a divided opinion inside us – the angel on one shoulder, the devil on the other. But not every decision needs debate, and not every decision is as binary as good versus bad.
- **Be empowered by the fact that you have choice over which thoughts you pursue.** They aren't just happening to you. You have control over which ones to indulge, and which ones to label.
- **Practise zooming out.** The further away you are from the issue at hand, the easier it is to be objective in your decision-making.
- **Take a pause.** Slowing down the process of reactive decision-making enables you to create distance between the action and the thought. Running thoughts require fast loops. Slowing them down creates space for you to think.
- **Identify what the strongest version of you would decide.** The more you visualise the person you want

to be, the easier it is to make decisions from a position of strength. What would a smart person do?

- **Fuck the ANTs.** ANTs are automatic negative thoughts. Fuck them off, they are an ingrained response and shouldn't be viewed as any more important than any other thoughts.
- **Make sure you are tracking the circumstances under which you're experiencing these unhelpful thoughts.** Do they occur at a certain time of day, in a particular environment, when you're with a certain group of people? Are you setting yourself up to win, matching your energy with the task, and creating the right environment for you to thrive?
- **Remember that there are three sides to every story:** Mine, yours, and the truth. Consider your opinion today, the automatic response that you've learned from the people around you, and what your best friend would say.
- **Return to reframing.** You're in control of the picture you paint.

ENDORPHINS

Have you ever experienced runner's high? No, me neither. But I have it on good authority from the runners I know that there exists a euphoric, sustained feeling at some point in a run that floods your system with endorphins and makes you feel as though you have a superpower. I believe that moment lies precisely five minutes after I stop running. Although the Chatty Cathys in the local running club will boast about chasing the runner's high, what's really going on is that your brain is releasing dopamine, you're getting lots of endorphins, and it's all mimicking the same addictive adrenaline that comes with taking class-A drugs.

Something similar can happen at work. Have you ever felt that time has flown by, that you're highly engaged with your work, no distraction will blow you off course, and you power through even the most challenging work task? Sounds like you've experienced Smart Flow, a positive mental state in which you are fully immersed in an activity, with full focus, energy and a high vibrational frequency. In other words, you get shit done.

Unfortunately, this state also zaps your energy. In fact, you can experience a 'flow comedown' afterwards, as you've used up all your juice for the day. As we learned on page 32, it's important to track your energy, not your time. This is particularly relevant here, given that working in a state of flow is a one-way ticket to using up most of your energy for the day.

Momentum is not represented by a headlong sprint towards your goals. It's slower than that. It's exciting to get things done, to feel as though you are progressing and pushing boundaries and challenging yourself. I'll *never* tell you to be less ambitious or less committed to your goals. I will, however, ask you to consider the state of your ecosystem, your fish tank, your car engine – all of these things require a regular thorough, accurate, honest and thoughtful health check in order to keep functioning.

Approval *Addiction*

One of the most important lessons I can teach you is to understand your own boundaries and dismantle your connection to approval addiction.

Approval addiction tends to occur in situations where we are directly being measured by our performance – at work, for example – and it involves becoming addicted to approval or praise, such as someone saying, 'Well done,' or 'You saved the day,' or a 'What would this team do without you?' Much like other forms of addiction, we can create unhealthy habits as we look for the next validated fix. This reliance on praise means that you increase the amount you seek it, and may feel low, empty and as though you're not in a state of flow without it. This is a one-way ticket to burnout, as you keep seeking more and more approval hits, running tasks into each other, taking on too much, and focusing disproportionately on what others think. It is also linked to a scarcity mindset, in which we are taught to focus on what we lack, that the amount of opportunity in the world is finite, that the success of others detracts from our own and that, ultimately, we're not truly good enough to achieve our goals.

Approval addiction produces negative momentum. If you aren't sure whether this is you, see if you connect with more than two of these points:

- You never seem to have enough time, cutting corners, working on a weekend but not logging it on your timesheets, turning up to work with wet hair.

- Meetings that would usually be routine begin to cause you anxiety.
- All feedback makes you feel unworthy, irrespective of whether it is positive or negative.
- Your friends label you as a high achiever but you feel on edge the entire time.
- The fear of failure plays on a loop inside your head.
- You don't enjoy the moment, as you are thinking of the next task.
- You say yes to everything, even if you know you can't do it.
- You like that people say you are reliable and work harder than anyone else.
- You admire those with extreme success stories.

Let's look at how you can steer yourself away from this and towards positive momentum:

- Re-evaluate why you place so much value on approval from others.
- Remind yourself of what is important to you, e.g. feeling safe, being seen, and think about other ways you could achieve these things.
- Work on why your level of productivity dictates your level of self-worth.
- Embrace and try to understand the fear you have. It's often rooted in not feeling good enough.
- Implement work–life boundaries that show others how to interact with you.

- Write down your values, and why they are important to you.
- Be more connected to the process, rather than the outcome.
- Surround yourself with people who make you feel fabulous.
- Edit your social media feed to ensure that you are viewing positive, inspiring and exciting content.
- Communicate. Let your manager or client know how you work best, what you need from them, and how to get the most out of the partnership.

When I was younger, I obsessed over the entrepreneurs who burned out, never saw their families and gave their lives to their companies. Now, the people I respect most are those who leave the office in good time, who have breakfast and make space for a balanced life. It's not about always working on the weekend, pulling an all-nighter and taking Pro Plus. It's about nurturing yourself so that you can be the happiest, most abundant version of you. You can't change the actions of other people; rather, you can focus on being the best version of yourself, and hope that inspires the same in others.

CONCLUSION

At this wordy juncture, you must confront the ingrained feeling that the harder the task is, the more successful you are. The longer you graft, practise, show up and study, the easier it will get. Of course, where we overcome a difficult pitch, hard conversation or relentless physical challenge, there is reward, but it's the steepness of the gradient, the breathlessness of the climb, that makes the view at the top even more rewarding.

I walked through much of my life stopping, picking up pebbles and placing them in my bag. The heavier my bag grew, the harder the climb became. Although I became fitter and stronger, I was demotivated. Everything felt hard and heavy. A therapist explained to me that I didn't have to carry the pebbles with me forever. I could learn from them, remember them, be grateful for them, hate them or feel connected to them, but I didn't have to *carry* them. The day that I finally set my bag down, took out the pebbles and carried on, was a momentous day. I know where they are, I just don't need them on the next part of my journey. And guess what? The climb is easier.

The same goes for living smarter. The reality of being a high achiever is that it's not smooth sailing all the time. In competitive sports, outcomes vary. Some days you deliver a personal best. Others, you're stiff and sore and slow. Your situation, and the environment you're in, will eternally evolve, shift and shape. The consistency that you can commit to is simply that you show up on all of those days. You need to challenge the idea that every shot must be on target, every pitch must be a win, every presentation delivered perfectly and every race a personal best. Letting go of your relationship with your perception of success is the first step towards living and working smarter.

I believe this to be the most valuable lesson, and it lies at the heart of the Smarter Method: smart people understand – and believe – that they are deserving of choice. They can choose to say no, to ask for more, to take the dance class, to meal-prep on a Sunday, to create a million-pound company. It is not the difficulty of the situation that dictates the outcome. It is how we choose to handle the situation, to face it, to overcome it. So often in films, literature and history, we have been led to believe we do not have choice. I spent much of my life resenting the idea that things were *happening to me*. I felt as though I was always on the back foot, that I was unlucky, and that I would be left on the bench, even after the stadium lights had been turned off. I accepted abusive relationships, allowed bad behaviour, was paid less than I deserved, inconvenienced myself for the benefit of others, and put myself last, for fear of rejection, judgement and shame. As I grew to understand the themes covered in this book, I implemented these ten lessons into my own life, providing myself with the freedom that I now have, and the confidence to show up for myself and to be big.

So, be big, even when you feel like the world wants you to be small, insignificant, one of many. Be loud when the world wants to silence you. Be strong when the pressure stands to weaken you, and feel light, even when the darkness seeps in. Our lives can often feel heavy, and the pressure we feel to achieve everything all at once is overwhelming. Burnout is paralysing and the nausea of wanting to succeed can dominate our thoughts and our physical bodies. My hope is that by reading this book, and taking its practical lessons with you, it might all seem more manageable. I wish for you to live an abundant life, one that is full (not just busy). One in which you have the confidence to centre yourself, ask for the things you want and set boundaries that protect you. I want you to feel brave, and enjoy a life that you have defined, on your own terms. I hope that you will achieve all that you want, by adopting a smarter way of living and working.

I do not want my legacy to be that of 'the tired woman'. I do not want to be remembered for always being late, stressed, busy and exhausted. I want to be someone who lives abundantly. A woman with a connection to my values and an ability to set and maintain healthy boundaries. A life in which success is not defined by how late I stay in the office, whether I performatively rise before 5am, whether I choose to miss important days or how often I post about my job online. A truly smarter life is one in which putting myself first is not selfish. One where I don't have to be 100 per cent sure all the time. One where I can be determined, ambitious and successful, most of the time. One where softness is not weakness, and one where I create my own definitions, with the courage to change things if they no longer serve me. I don't believe it to be easy, but I do believe there is evidence all around us that it is possible. I'd like my legacy to be that I was part of that evidence.

ACKNOWLEDGEMENTS

To Morwenna, thank you for guiding me through this process from start to finish.

To Jill, the best editor I could have wished for. To Jill, Stephanie, Lucie and the team at Hachette for believing in *Smarter* and supporting women in pursuit of achieving more.

To Freddie, Daisy, Caite and Roxie for proofreading, listening, helping and thinking.

To my Jon, for selflessly building me up to be the best version of myself. Walking behind me to push me on, in front of me to show me where to go, and beside me in our chosen team of two.

To my family at EMERGE: thank you to each and every one of you for allowing me to show up every day and live out my career dreams. Thanks especially to Mel, Lauren and Ashleigh – thank you for helping me bring *Smarter* to life. To Steph, for creating Smarter in a way I could never have imagined. You are a branding genius.

NOTES

CHAPTER 1: MORNINGS

1. National Institute of General Medical Sciences. 'Circadian rhythms'. www.nigms.nih.gov.
2. National Institute of General Medical Sciences. 'Circadian rhythms'. www.nigms.nih.gov.
3. Bloomberg Television. 'Amazon's Bezos says three good decisions a day "enough"' [video]. 20 September 2018. www.youtube.com.
4. Kracow, E. 'How many decisions do we make each day?' 27 September 2018. www.psychologytoday.com.
5. Lark. 'Decision fatigue: Understanding its impact on productivity'. 22 December 2023. www.larksuite.com.
6. Denham Smith, D. 'How to make decision fatigue more bearable'. 8 September 2022. www.fastcompany.com.
7. Swns Digital. 'The average Brit makes 122 decisions a day, with 87 per cent often changing their mind'. 9 August 2022. www.swnsdigital.com.

CHAPTER 2: MESSAGE

1. Hayashi, Alden M. 'When to Trust Your Gut'. *Harvard Business Review*. February 2001.

CHAPTER 5: MANAGE

1. Maw, A. 'Multitasking is out, monotasking is in'. 24 October 2023. www.jotform.com.
2. Cloninger, C. R., Svrakic, D. M., Przybeck, T.R. 'A psychobiological model of temperament and character'. *Archives of General Psychiatry*. December 1993. 50(12):975–90.
3. Krebs, E. E., Lorenz, K. A., Bair, M. J., Damush, T. M., Wu, J., Sutherland, J. M., Asch, S. M., Kroenke, K. 'Development and initial validation of the PEG, a three-item scale assessing pain intensity and interference'. *Journal of General Internal Medicine*. June 2009. 24(6):733–8.
4. Naeem, M., Ozuem, W., Howell, K., & Ranfagni, S. 'A Step-by-Step Process of Thematic Analysis to Develop a Conceptual Model in Qualitative Research'. *International Journal of Qualitative Methods*. 2023. 22.

CHAPTER 6: MODIFY

1. Chang, R. 'How to make hard choices' [video]. May 2014. ww.ted.com.
2. Visier Team, 'Quick, act busy! New Research shows many workers admit to "productivity theatre"'. www.visier.com/blog/productivity-survey-shows-performative-work.
3. Tseng, J., Poppenk, J. 'Brain meta-state transitions demarcate thoughts across task contexts exposing the mental noise of trait neuroticism'. *Nature Communications*. 11, 3480 (2020).

CHAPTER 9: MOVE

1. Wooll, M. 'How to hold yourself accountable: 5 tips to start today'. 11 November 2022. www.betterup.com.
2. Lewis, R. 'The brain as a prediction machine: The key to consciousness?' 1 January 2022. www.psychologytoday.com.
3. Seth, A. 'Your brain hallucinates your conscious reality' [video]. April 2017. www.ted.com.

CHAPTER 10: MOMENTUM

1. Nickerson, C. 'Zeigarnik effect examples in psychology'. 26 October 2023. www.simplypsychology.org.
2. Solan, M. 'Calming and refocusing when anxious or negative thoughts surge through your mind'. 13 March 2023, www.health.harvard.edu.

INDEX

Abercrombie, 3
abundance, 5, 9, 10, 55–6, 63–9, 100, 103, 194, 259
  hype women and, 135, 136
  personal brand and, 187
  self-talk and, 70
  space for everyone, 126, 197
  variety and, 79
accountability, 69, 78, 83, 87, 92, 115, 224–6, 234
addictions, 196
advice, 245–7
al-Ajroush, Madeha, 131
altruistic behaviour, 53–4, 208
Amazon, 39
ambition, 1, 4, 5, 26, 56, 91, 135, 176, 188, 190, 196
  accountability and, 224
  vision boards and, 181–2
Amos, Valerie, 133
Angelou, Maya, 55
anxiety, 15, 19, 46–7, 50, 63, 67, 199, 201, 208, 242, 255
  catastrophising, 137, 247–8
  imposter syndrome and, 121
  perception and, 228, 230
  task tension and, 238
apathy, 14, 40, 242
appetite loss, 15
approval addiction, 254–6
arena vs stands, 188–90
Atlas of the Heart (Brown), 62
Atomic Habits (Clear), 58, 180
audio, 28, 32, 78, 206, 223
automatic negative thoughts (ANTs), 252

balance, 36, 168
baths, 19, 52, 61, 207, 223
Beckham, David, 28
Beecher, Henry Ward, 26
Being You (Seth), 228

Beyoncé, 136
Bezos, Jeff, 39, 42
Bigelow, Kathryn, 132
biological prime time, 37
Blakely, Sara, 45, 181
bottom-up approach, 158–9
boundaries, 5, 86, 92–113, 255
  accountability and, 226
  crossing of, 107–8
  five types, 98
  hard and soft, 104
  non-negotiables, 109–12
  online, 109
  people-pleasing and, 117
  productivity theatre and, 179
  social media and, 191
  values and, 100–103
Brown, Brené, 62, 69, 188, 190, 198
burnout, 4, 6, 7, 13–19, 26, 29, 35, 176, 182, 195, 209, 242, 259
  approval addiction and 254
  decision fatigue, 14, 42
  exercise and, 219
  habit diaries, 16–18
  motivation and, 26
  signs of, 13–15, 26
  time management and, 82
  urgent vs important, 35–6
busyness, 175, 185, 194, 196, 198–200, 259
  detoxing, 91, 204–8, 243

caffeine, 21, 22, 222
Carpenter, Sam, 37
Carr, Jo, 60
catastrophising, 137, 247–8
certainty, 74–5
challenges
  approach to, 9
  mental resilience and, 125
  overcoming of, 46–7
champagne glass analogy, 240–41
Chanel, Coco, 119
Chang, Ruth, 165
changing thought patterns, 249–52
Cherokee wolf legend, 62–3
circadian rhythms, 22–4, 30
circles, 237
Cirillo, Francesco, 87
Clear, James, 58, 180
coffee, 11, 31, 53, 112, 127, 149, 152, 183, 215
cognitive behavioural therapy (CBT), 249
cognitive reframing, *see* reframing
comparisons, 25, 65, 129, 130, 189
compassion, 5, 66, 96, 124, 209, 226
concentration, 34, 65, 85–6, 92
confidence, 62, 96, 98, 126, 129, 136
consumerism, 208
Covey, Stephen, 140
Covid-19 pandemic (2019–23), 4, 19, 177, 248
creativity, 34, 39, 42, 111, 122, 152, 199
Cunningham, Stacey, 131

Daily Dos, 182–4
Daring Greatly (Brown), 69, 188, 190, 198
deadlines, 81, 82, 91, 147, 243
decision-making, 27–9, 39–45, 161–73
  certainty and, 74–5
  emotion vs logic, 162–4
  fatigue and, 14, 42

novelty bias, 140, 156–8
pros and cons, 165–6
three Cs, 41
three good decisions, 39, 42
definitions, 5, 13, 147, 210–13, 245
delegation, 87, 150–53, 159, 160
depression, 4
desk timers, 85–6, 144, 157
Diet Coke, 215
diet, *see* eating habits
discipline, 47, 169, 199, 225
Ditching Imposter Syndrome (Josa), 116
dopamine, 156, 196, 253
doubling it, 218–20
Dropbox, 244
Duffy, Carol Ann, 133

eating habits, 7, 16, 26, 38, 112, 183, 207, 219, 220
lunch, 18, 22, 38, 177
overeating, 195, 231
sluggishness and, 38
Ederle, Gertrude, 132
ego, 129–30
eight-hour days, 32
Eisenhower Matrix, 148
elimination or delegation, 87, 150–53, 159, 160
emails, 30, 31, 48, 49, 125, 151, 156, 177
emotional capacity, 124
emotional intelligence, 111, 124
emotional reactions, 162–4
empathy, 103, 124
endorphins, 252–3
energy, 5, 32–42, 43, 45, 46, 66, 76, 130, 159, 214
attraction of, 68, 135
busyness and, 196, 198
catastrophising and, 247–8
logic and, 163
novelty bias and, 157
task management and, 141, 143, 144, 148, 159, 171, 214, 238, 252
time and, 5, 32–42, 50, 52, 81, 83, 88, 144, 179, 253
environment checks, 149, 159
EQ (emotional quotient), 111, 124
equilibrium, 36, 161, 167–8
essentials and luxuries, 110–12
exercise, 21, 22, 25, 26, 41, 125, 195, 210, 217–20

failure, 60, 64, 119, 128, 139, 174, 211, 233, 244–5
fear of, 76, 117, 131, 220, 222, 255
setting up for, 147, 159, 243
family life, 7, 9, 76, 127, 166, 167, 223
fatigue, 15
feminism, 6, 213
fight-or-flight response, 247–8
finishing the thought, 248–9
fish tank, 168–70
Fitzgerald, Ella, 132
flow, 5, 37, 50, 90, 236, 238–9, 253
Ford, Henry, 161
four Ds, 151
four Ps, 116–18

glass ceilings, 130–34
goal setting, 56, 58, 59–60, 117, 129
SMART goals, 226–30
vision boards, 180–82
going ghost, 191–3

Google Street View, 28
gratitude, 5, 66, 69, 95, 128, 130
Grind, 3
grounded confidence, 62
growth mindset, 135, 138–9
gut health, 220
gut instinct, 70–74, 116, 122, 163, 191, 201
gyms, *see* exercise

habits, 169, 231–5
  diaries, 16–18
  pairing, 144–6, 223
  to-don't list, 210, 214–17
Harris, Ben, 178
Harry Potter audiobooks, 28, 206, 223
headphones, 53, 112
HMRC, 18
Hope & Glory, 60
House of Lords, 132, 133
Houston, Drew, 244
Huel, 3
Hunt-Davis, Ben, 203
hybrid working, 177
hygiene, 169
hype woman, 62, 115, 134–9
hyperfocus, 37, 60, 169, 195
hypnotherapy, 56, 57, 249

identity, 58–60
imposter syndrome, 114–24
  embracement of, 120
  four Ps, 116–18
  management, 119–20, 123
  as positive, 118–19
Indy Japan 300, 132
inner voice, 61–3, 64, 66, 69–70, 115, 134–9
Instagram, 177, 193, 247

Jemison, Mae, 131
Jobs, Steve, 20, 41
Josa, Clare, 116

Kennedy, John Fitzgerald, 174
kindness, 62–3, 220

labels, 137–8
language, 69–70
law of assumption, 159
Lewis, Ralph, 228
Liberia, 131
libido, 13
life perspectives, 158–60
LinkedIn, 30, 84, 185, 187, 193
literature, 78
Loehr, Jim, 37, 38
logical reactions, 162–4
Lovelace, Ada, 132
lunch, 18, 22, 38, 177
luxuries, 110–12
lying, 20–22, 204

maintenance, 169
make-up, 222, 223
Maltz, Maxwell, 128
'Man in the Arena, The' (Roosevelt), 188
Manifest (Nafousi), 58
manifesting, 56, 57, 169
marketing, 174–93
  arena vs stands, 188–90
  Daily Dos, 182–4

personal brand, 185–8
productivity theatre, 176–9
vision boards, 179–82
Massachusetts Institute of Technology, 121
McKinsey, 7
McWilliams, Monica, 131
Medhurst, Leeson, 178
meditation, 25, 47, 56, 207, 223
mental health, 7, 61–3, 68, 97, 175
mental resilience, 124–34
mentors, 245–7
micro changes, 162
mindfulness, 103, 125
momentum, 5, 236–56
approval addiction and, 254–6
catastrophising, 247–8
champagne glass analogy, 240–41
changing thought patterns, 249–52
direction, 241–4
endorphins and, 252–3
failure and, 244–5
finishing the thought, 248–9
mentoring and, 245–7
task tension, 238–9
task, ask, action, 239–40
mono-tasking, 90, 140, 141–4, 207, 239
mornings, 5, 11–54
achievement, 26–7
altruistic behaviour and, 53–4
burnout and, 13–19
challenges, overcoming of, 46–7
circadian rhythms and, 22–4, 30
decision-making and, 27–9, 39–45
energy vs time tracking, 32–9
5am club, 21, 222
lying about, 20–22
phones and, 30–32
priority lists, 45–6
procrastination and, 48–53
routines, 25
showing up, 12–13
snooze button and, 21, 29
motherhood, 10, 242
motivation, 26
Mount Everest, 133
multitasking, 140, 141–4, 145, 148, 237
music, 28, 78

Nafousi, Roxie, 58
natural abilities, 196
natural energy, 13, 34, 39
nausea, 15
negativity, 64, 66, 117, 121, 125, 130, 135
ANTs, 252
bias towards, 137
law of assumption and, 159
paralysis and, 117–18
reframing, 46–7, 201–2
New York Stock Exchange, 131
Nike, 185–6
non-negotiables, 109–12
Noom, 40
Northern Ireland Women's Coalition, 131
novelty bias, 140, 156–8
numbing behaviours, 198

OCD (obsessive compulsive disorder), 4, 249

Olympic Games, 181, 203
optical illusions, 229
other-orientation, 122–3

paralysis, 117–18
Patrick, Danica, 132
pay, 67, 96, 93, 95, 105, 130, 154, 189
Peck, M. Scott, 80
Peldon Rose, 178
people-pleasing, 117
perfectionism, 117
personal brand, 185–8
personal trainers, 25, 218, 220, 239
perspectives on life, 158–60
Phillips, Bill, 210
phones, 30–32, 47, 86, 149, 191, 206, 215, 223
pie charts, 84, 166
Pilates, 127, 215, 219
podcasts, 78, 183, 207, 244, 246
pomodoro technique, 87
positivity, 9, 38, 46–7, 62, 125, 137, 160
Post-it notes, 177
power hour, 37
practice, 169
prediction machines, 228–30
priority lists, 45–6
procrastination, 45, 48–53, 118
productivity, 1, 8, 9
  boundaries and, 80
  busyness and, 194, 204
  decision-making and, 42
  delegation and, 150, 170
  momentum and, 237
  mono-tasking and, 142
  procrastination and, 45, 48
  self-worth and, 144, 255
  sleep and, 222
  ten-second test, 48
  theatre of, 176–9
  time-management and, 32, 87
  to-don't lists and, 214, 217
productivity theatre, 176–9
property market, 94
pros and cons, 165–6
psycho-cybernetics, 114, 128–34
PTSD (post-traumatic stress disorder), 4
purposefulness, 125

Queen's University, 201

RACI, 170–73
Red Bull, 3
reframing, 8, 9, 46, 121, 194, 200–203, 252
  decision-making, 161–73
  exercise and, 218–20
  imposter syndrome, 117–18, 121
  mornings, 26, 46
  showing up, 12
  success vs pain, 183–4
  time management, 82
relationships, 63, 66, 68–9, 77, 93, 105, 125, 158, 163, 256
  romantic, 9, 101, 130, 164, 167
remote working, 177
resilience, 124–34
Rogers, Will, 236
romantic relationships, 9, 101, 130, 164, 167
Roosevelt, Theodore, 188

Rubenstein, David, 39
running, 253

Saudi Arabia, 131
scarcity mindset, 64–5, 130, 194, 195
Secret Thoughts of Successful Women, The (Young) 122
self-awareness, 125
self-care, 52, 61, 64, 117, 125, 183
self-compassion, 66, 226
self-confidence, 62, 96, 98, 126, 129, 136
self-destructiveness, 195
self-discipline, 47, 169, 199, 225
self-doubt, 63, 76, 115, 117, 118, 120, 121, 238, 242, 246
self-editing, 5
self-esteem, 61, 65, 96, 98, 130
self-fulfilling prophecies, 60
self-image, 128–34
self-promotion, 114, 126–8
self-sabotage, 60
self-talk, 61–3, 64, 66, 69–70, 115, 134–9
self-worth, 1, 61, 117, 144, 255
Seth, Anil, 228, 229
setting up to win, 135, 180, 197, 206
Seven Summits, 133
sex, 13
showing up, 3, 12–13
Sirleaf, Ellen Johnson, 131
Slack, 30, 48, 52, 177
sleep, 15, 210, 220–24
  bedtime routines, 30, 39, 57, 183, 223
  circadian rhythms, 22–4, 30
  early rising, 21, 222
  snooze button and, 21, 29
Sleep Foundation, 23
sluggishness, 22, 23, 34, 38
Smart Flow, 253
SMART goals, 226–30
smartphones, *see* phones
smoking, 58–9, 196
Snapchat, 193
Snicket, Lemony, 11
social media, 2, 18, 46, 84, 149, 191–3, 175, 222, 246–7, 256
  addiction to, 175
  comparisons and, 25, 222
  going ghost, 191–3
  personal branding and, 186
  productivity theatre, 177–8
  self-promotion, 127–8
  sleep and, 31, 223
  to-don't lists and, 215, 217
socialising, 14, 195, 206
solution-orientation, 111, 122
Spanx, 3, 45, 181
sticky floors, 133–4
Stop, Start, Continue Framework, 140, 150, 153–5, 160
stress, 15, 19, 46–7, 49, 259
  abundance and, 64
  anticipatory, 46
  catastrophising and, 137, 247
  hype woman and, 67
  imposter syndrome and, 116
  time-management and, 82
  to-do lists and, 214
Swanborough, Stella Isaacs, Baroness, 132

task, ask, action, 239–40
task tension, 238–9

teamwork, 103
tears, 15
ten-second test, 48
Thatcher, Margaret, 7
thought patterns, changing of, 249–52
three good decisions, 39, 42
tidying your room, 181
TikTok, 15, 30, 156, 178, 193, 215
time; time management, 32, 80–113, 140
  activities vs results, 82
  boundaries and, 86, 92–113
  elimination or delegation, 87, 150–53, 159, 160
  energy and, 5, 32–42, 50, 52, 81, 83, 88, 144, 179, 253
  four Ds, 151
  480-minute day, 90–92
  pie charts, 84
  pomodoro technique, 87
  time-blocking, 87–92
  timers, 85–7
  tracking, 83–5
timers, 85–7, 144, 157
to-don't lists, 210, 214–17, 232
tolerance, lack of, 14
top-down approach, 158–9

University of Salzburg, 121
University of Toronto, 228
urgent vs important, 35–6, 146–8, 159

values, 5, 166, 256
  accountability and, 226
  boundaries and, 99, 100–103
  decision-making and, 166
  non-negotiables and, 110
  self-promotion and, 127–8
variety, 77–9
victor bias, 181
virtue signalling, 129
Visier, 176, 178
vision boards, 179–82
visualisation, 56–60, 138, 166, 179

Wahlberg, Mark, 25
Webb, Keith, 194
weight; weight loss, 3, 130, 184, 208, 213, 218
WhatsApp, 49, 162
Will It Make the Boat Go Faster? (Hunt-Davis), 130, 150, 203, 204, 205, 241, 243
Williams, Venus, 57
Winfrey, Oprah, 181–2
winning, setting up for, 135, 180, 197, 206
Witherspoon, Reese, 182
women, 6–8, 63, 130–34, 197, 209, 245
  glass ceilings, 130–34
  imposter syndrome and, 116, 117, 120–21
  motherhood, 10, 242
Wooll, Maggie, 225
Work the System (Carpenter), 37
work–life balance, 9
working lunches, 177

yoga, 207
Young, Valerie, 122

Zeigarnik Effect, 238